Business Perspective: The IS View on Delivering Services to the Business

Office of Government Commerce

ITIL® Managing IT services

London: TSO

Published by TSO (The Stationery Office) and available from:

Online
www.tso.co.uk/bookshop

Mail, Telephone, Fax & E-mail
TSO
PO Box 29, Norwich, NR3 1GN
Telephone orders/General enquiries: 0870 600 5522
Fax orders: 0870 600 5533
E-mail: book.orders@tso.co.uk
Textphone 0870 240 3701

TSO Shops
123 Kingsway, London, WC2B 6PQ
020 7242 6393 Fax 020 7242 6394
68-69 Bull Street, Birmingham B4 6AD
0121 236 9696 Fax 0121 236 9699
9-21 Princess Street, Manchester M60 8AS
0161 834 7201 Fax 0161 833 0634
16 Arthur Street, Belfast BT1 4GD
028 9023 8451 Fax 028 9023 5401
18-19 High Street, Cardiff CF10 1PT
029 2039 5548 Fax 029 2038 4347
71 Lothian Road, Edinburgh EH3 9AZ
0870 606 5566 Fax 0870 606 5588

TSO Accredited Agents
(see Yellow Pages)

and through good booksellers

For further information on OGC products, contact:

OGC Service Desk
Rosebery Court
St Andrews Business Park
Norwich NR7 0HS
Telephone +44 (0) 845 000 4999

First published 2004
Second Impression 2005
ISBN 0 11 330894 9

Printed in the United Kingdom for The Stationery Office
ID177091   C50   03/05   301078

Titles within the ITIL series include:

Service Support (Published 2000)
Service Desk and the Process of Incident
Management, Problem Management, Configuration
Management, Change Management and
Release Management   ISBN 0 11 330015 8

Service Delivery (Published 2001)
Capacity Management, Availability Management,
Service Level Management, IT Service Continuity,
Finanacial Management for IT Services and
Customer Relationship Management   ISBN 0 11 330017 4

ICT Infrastructure Management   ISBN 0 11 330865 5
Application Management   ISBN 0 11 330866 3
Planning to Implement Service Management ISBN 0 11 330877 9
Security Management   ISBN 0 11 330014 X

ITIL back catalogue – an historical repository available as PDF downloads from www.tso.co.uk/ITIL

The managers' set
The complementary guidance set
Environmental management, strategy and computer operations set

■ CONTENTS

FOREWORD

Organisations are increasingly dependent on electronic delivery of services to meet customer needs. This means a requirement for high-quality Information Systems (IS) services, matched to business needs and user requirements as they evolve.

OGC's ITIL (IT Infrastructure Library) is the most widely accepted approach to IT Service Management in the world. ITIL provides a cohesive set of best practices, drawn from the public and private sectors internationally, supported by a comprehensive qualification scheme, accredited training organisations, and implementation and assessment tools.

Bob Assirati

OGC

PREFACE

The ethos behind the development of ITIL (IT Infrastructure Library) is the recognition that organisations are increasingly dependent upon Information Systems (IS) to satisfy their corporate aims and meet their business needs. This growing dependency leads to greater needs for quality IS services – quality that is matched to business needs and user requirements as they emerge.

This is true no matter what type or size of organisation, be it national government, a multinational conglomerate, a decentralised office with either a local or centralised IS provision, an outsourced service provider, or a single office environment with one person providing IS support. In each case there is the requirement to provide an economical service that is reliable, consistent and fit for purpose.

IT Service Management is concerned with delivering and supporting IS services that are appropriate to the business requirements of the organisation. ITIL provides a comprehensive, consistent and coherent set of best practices for IT Service Management processes, promoting a quality approach to achieving business effectiveness and efficiency in the use of information systems. ITIL Service Management processes are intended to be implemented so that they underpin but do not dictate the business processes of an organisation. IS service providers will be striving to improve the quality of the service, but at the same time they will be trying to reduce the costs or, at a minimum, maintain costs at the current level.

The best practice processes promoted in this book both support and are supported by the British Standards Institution's Standard for IT Service Management (BS 15000), and the ISO quality standard ISO 9000.

The authors

The guidance in this book was distilled from the experience of a range of authors working in the private sector in IT Service Management. The material was written by:

Graham Dawson	Fujitsu Services
Gerry Gough	Fujitsu Services
Ashley Hanna	Hewlett-Packard
Gary Hodgkiss	Capgemini
Vernon Lloyd	Fox IT
Ivor Macfarlane	Guillemot Rock Ltd
Bruce Pinnington	Essential Consultancy Services Ltd
Vera Rodrigues	Fujitsu Services
Colin Rudd	itEMS Ltd
Sue Shaw	TriCentrica
Sharon Taylor	Aspect Group Inc

With contributions from:

John Gibert	Southcourt Ltd
Gerry McLaughlin	Fox IT
John Windebank	Mongoose Consulting

Editor

Alison Cartlidge   Xansa

Project Manager

Chris Lang   *it*SMF

Reviewers

A wide-ranging national and international Quality Assurance (QA) exercise was carried out by people proposed by OGC and *it*SMF. OGC and *it*SMF wish to express their particular appreciation to the following people who spent considerable time and effort (far beyond the call of duty!) on QA of the material:

David D'Agostino	Peregrine Systems
Bob Arthars	QH & NSWH Oral Health
Graham Barnett	Fujitsu Services
Marc Baumgart	DCON Software & Service AG
Hans Van Den Bent	PinkRoccade IT Management
Bernd Broksch	Siemens Business Services GmbH & Co. OHG
Brian Broadhurst	Fox IT
Derek Cambray	Fujitsu Services
Ole Vidar Christensen	NDLO/CIS (Norwegian Defence Logistics Organisation/ Communication Information Services)
Bernd Drollinger	dv-werk gmbh
Simone Fuchs	SAP AG
Karen Ferris	KMF Advance
John Groom	WGC
Louis van Hemmen	BITALL b.v.
Sandra Hendriks	
Signe Marie Hernes	Det Norske Veritas (DNV)
Dave Hinley	DS Hinley Associates
Björn Hinrichs	SITGATE AG
Steve Ingall	Fox IT
Roar Johnsen	Ciber Norway
Chris Jones	Ariston Strategic Consulting
Peter Joy	Fujitsu Services
Adrian Leach	Parity
Colin Lovell	Hewlett-Packard
Paul Martini	Peregrine Systems
Gaetan Maugin	Axios Systems
Christian Probst	
Rodica Radulescu	ifm electronic GmbH
Stuart Rance	Hewlett-Packard
Martin Rother	Management Methods
Jane Seeley	Exel Logistics
Andreas Stremel	Siemens Business Services GmbH & Co. OHG
Bridget Veitch	Xansa
Dave Ward	IBM Global Services
Alan White	ProActive Services Pty Ltd

Contact information

Full details of the range of material published under the ITIL banner can be found at www.itil.co.uk.

For further information on this and other OGC products, please visit the OGC website at www.ogc.gov.uk. Alternatively, please contact:

OGC Service Desk
Rosebery Court
St Andrews Business Park
Norwich
NR7 0HS
United Kingdom
Tel: +44 (0) 845 000 4999
Email: info@ogc.gov.uk

1 INTRODUCTION

1.1 Aim of this book

The increasingly important contribution of IT to the success – or failure – of a business is an established fact. Without it, very few businesses would be able to stay competitive. Likewise, it is difficult to see how most public sector organisations could demonstrate value in the delivery of their services.

Despite this, the relationship between Information Systems (IS) and the rest of the organisation that it serves can often appear to be in need of counselling. It has been estimated that the success rate of IS projects to deliver new services is as low as 30%, and there have been numerous embarrassing and spectacular examples in the media of problems caused – or apparently caused – by the failings of the IS community. The risk of a costly failure is a recurring concern for many senior managers, both inside and outside of IS, yet this risk can be effectively and significantly reduced by adopting a Business Perspective.

Typical business managers spend their time thinking from the perspective of the balance sheet, the profit and loss statement or number of units shipped. For IS to adopt a Business Perspective they need to view their service through the same filter.

Within the ITIL framework, the aim of this *Business Perspective* book is to help create that awareness for IT practitioners, about the key principles and requirements of the business organisation and their operation, and how these relate to the development, delivery and support of IS services. This awareness of business needs enables IS to establish the most effective business aligned relationships, interfaces and service delivery, so maximising the business benefit that can be realised by IS and the quality of services delivered.

The objectives of this *Business Perspective* book are to equip readers with the knowledge to:

- enable IS personnel to:
  - understand how they contribute to business objectives
  - deliver and improve IS services to underpin business objectives
  - assist the business in maximising the exploitation of IS

- understand the need for a complementary and integrated culture with the business
- influence, innovate and enable change for business benefit.

This book builds on the foundations provided by *Service Support*, *Service Delivery*, *Application Management*, *Planning to Implement Service Management*, *Security Management* and *ICT Infrastructure Management*. It shows how the best practice described in these publications can be deployed with a business focus and extended and integrated into the business. This is essential, given that there is an absolute dependence of most businesses upon IS.

The book provides particular guidance on the following topics:

- **Establishing effective relationships at operational, tactical and strategic levels between the business, IS, and IS suppliers**: this enables effective and innovative use of IS, driven by and for business benefit, acting as an agent for change to support business transformation and meeting ever increasing, rapidly changing business demands.

■ **Aligning and continuing to align IS services to the needs of the business**: this includes assessing how the current approach to IS service provision is meeting the business's requirements and, if it is not, to outline the approach necessary to ensure that the IS service provision can and does meet the current and future needs of the business.

■ **Ensuring the quality of services delivered matches business expectations**: this includes synchronisation with the business drivers, aligning business and IS cultures and improving the quality of the experience for all business/IS or IS/customer touch points.

■ **Understanding the role of IS in the business value chain**: a better understanding of the business dependencies on IS improves realisation of tangible business benefits, optimisation of any investment in the Portfolio of Services and more business focused IS services, all delivered by business aware IS resource.

■ **Identifying how IS delivers business value**: this enables IS to better demonstrate to their business the value of the services being delivered and how that value can improve with future IS developments. If IS has a clear understanding of how it delivers value to each Business Unit, it is better able to market its capabilities and further expand the usage of its services.

■ **Understanding the business view point**: understanding how the business views the services they use and the context in which they use those services enables IS to contribute more effectively to the delivery of business processes.

■ **Using ITIL to develop integrated end-to-end processes across the business and IS**: this achieves the advantages of synergy and partnership across the entire business organisation. If IT Service Management processes are not implemented, managed and supported in the appropriate way within IS, the business will experience unacceptable degradation in terms of loss of productive hours, higher costs, loss of revenue or perhaps even business failure, depending upon the criticality of the IS service to the business.

■ **Differentiating between the roles of Business Relationship Management and Service Management**: this ensures clarity, and so effectiveness, in operation as the Service Delivery Manager and the Business Relationship Manager roles have very different responsibilities, interfaces and processes.

■ **Working with suppliers at all types and levels of engagement**: this considers working relationships, alignment of supplier services to business requirements and supply chain management to ensure these relationships underpin the overarching business needs and that these relationships are maximised to business benefit.

■ **Establishing and operating IS as a business within a business**: this ensures aspects such as polices and standards, governance, financial strategies, and performance management are in place and aligned to the overall corporate approach and business objectives, enabling IS to be see as demonstrably contributing to corporate goals and strategies and business development, rather than as an overhead or a function to be tolerated.

This book is one of a series issued as part of ITIL which documents industry best practice for the support and delivery of IS services. Although this book can be read in isolation, it is recommended that it be used in conjunction with the other ITIL books. The guidance contained within the book is also scaleable – applicable to both small and large organisations. It applies to distributed and centralised systems, whether developed in-house or supplied by third parties, and irrespective of how IS is delivered e.g. in-house, outsourced managed service or partnership arrangement. It is neither bureaucratic nor unwieldy if implemented sensibly and in full recognition of the business needs of the organisation.

1.2 Target audience

This book is relevant to anyone involved or associated with the delivery or support of IS services. It is particularly relevant to:

- Business Relationship Management (may also be known as Customer Relationship Management, Account Management, Client Management)
- Service Management
- Application Development Management
- Business Management interfacing with IS
- Supplier Management
- Contract Management
- Procurement/Purchasing Management
- Quality Management
- Business Continuity Management
- Risk Management.

It is difficult to think of any IS management for whom this book does not have some relevance, as this book provides access to proven best practice based on the experience and knowledge of experienced industry practitioners in adopting a Business Perspective approach to delivering Service Management.

Since everyone in IS needs to understand that they all interact with the business in some way, the key concepts and processes included in this book can be used to develop training and awareness programmes for all IS teams ensuring the delivery of services that are aligned to the business requirements, encompassing both tangible (e.g. service levels) and intangible (e.g. service culture) aspects.

For Business Managers there is value in understanding the interfaces with IS, enabling a more effective relationship and maximising the business value from IS.

This book is also relevant for managers of supplier organisations in understanding how they fit into an IS service delivery organisation and how they contribute to achieving business objectives.

1.3 ITIL

Developed from the late 1980s, ITIL has become the worldwide *de facto* standard in IT Service Management. Starting as a guide for UK government, the framework has proved to be useful to organisations in all sectors through its adoption by many Service Management companies as the basis for consultancy, education and software tools support. Today, ITIL is known and used worldwide.

The reasons for its success are explained in the remainder of this section.

1.3.1 Public domain framework

From the beginning, ITIL has been publicly available. This means that any organisation can use the framework described by the OGC in its numerous books. Because of this, a wide range of organisations including local and central government, energy, public utilities, retail, finance, and manufacturing have used ITIL guidance. Very large organisations, very small organisations and everything in between have implemented ITIL processes.

1.3.2 Best practice framework

ITIL documents industry best practice guidance. It has proved its value from the very beginning. Initially, OGC collected information on how various organisations addressed the provision of quality IS services, analysed this and filtered those issues that would prove useful to OGC and to its customers in UK central government. Other organisations found that the guidance was generally applicable and markets outside of government were very soon created by the service industry.

Being a framework, ITIL describes the contours of organising Service Management. The models show the goals, general activities, inputs and outputs of the various processes, which can be incorporated within IS organisations. ITIL does not cast in stone every action required on a day-to-day basis because that is something which differs from organisation to organisation. Instead it focuses on best practice that can be utilised in different ways according to need. Figure 1.1 shows the scope of ITIL and its individual elements.

Thanks to this framework of proven best practice, ITIL can be used within organisations with existing methods and activities. Using ITIL doesn't imply a completely new way of thinking and acting. It provides a framework in which to place existing methods and activities in a structured context. By emphasising the relationships between the processes, any lack of communication and co-operation between various IS functions can be minimised or eliminated.

ITIL provides a proven method for planning common processes, roles and activities with appropriate reference to each other and how the communication lines should function between them.

ITIL books detail industry best practice processes in all aspects of the delivery, support, provision and management of IS services. By using lessons learnt in the field this book gives practical guidance on the establishment and operation of an effective Business Perspective approach.

1.3.3 *De facto* standard

By the mid-1990s, ITIL was recognised as the world *de facto* standard for IT Service Management. A major advantage of a generally recognised method is a common vocabulary. The books define a large number of terms that, when used correctly, can help people to understand each other within IS organisations. They also help to communicate in terms that the business understands. One common complaint from the business community is that IS staff communicate in technology speak. ITIL helps remove the barriers and offers a common framework for communicating to the business community.

An important part of ITIL projects is getting people to speak that common language. That is why education is one of the essential items of an implementation or improvement programme. Only when the people involved use a common language can a project be successful.

1.3.4 Quality approach and standards

In the past, many IS organisations were internally focused and concentrated on technical issues. These days, businesses have high expectations towards the quality of services and these expectations change with time. This means that for IS organisations to live up to these expectations they need to concentrate on service quality and a more customer and business oriented approach. Cost issues are frequently high on the agenda, as is the development of a more business-like attitude to provision of service.

ITIL focuses on providing high quality services with a particular focus on business and customer relationships. This means that the IS organisation provides whatever is agreed with customers, which implies a strong relationship between the IS organisation and their customers, users and partners.

Service processes are centred on the relationships between the IS organisation and their customers. Service Delivery is principally concerned with setting up agreements and monitoring the targets within these agreements. Meanwhile, on the operational level, the Service Support and ICT Infrastructure Management processes can be viewed as delivering services as laid down within these agreements. On both levels there is a strong relationship with quality systems such as ISO 9000 and a total quality framework such as European Framework for Quality Management (EFQM). ITIL supports these quality systems by providing defined processes and best practice for the management of IS Services, enabling a fast track towards ISO certification. Attaining a quality standard is beneficial for organisations but it has to be recognised that this alone does not guarantee delivery of the service expected by the business. There would need to be ongoing review of quality of processes aligned with business requirements. There are several Total Quality Management (TQM) approaches to process improvement that are complemented by the use of ITIL; reference is made to most of these approaches in Appendix C.

The British Standards Institution (BSi) published *IT Service Management – A Manager's Guide* (BIP0005) which was based on the principles of ITIL and there is now a *British Standard for Service Management*, BS 15000-1:2002, and a *Code of Practice for Service Management*, BS 15000-2:2003, both of which have been derived from ITIL under a concordat between BSi, OGC and *it*SMF. Consequently, both BSi and OGC espouse similar, if not identical, principles of best practice for IT Service Management.

1.3.5 *it*SMF

The *it*SMF (IT Service Management Forum) was set up to support and influence the IT Service Management industry. It has, through its very large membership, been influential in promoting industry best practice and driving updates to ITIL.

1.4 The structure of ITIL

The concept of managing IS services for the improvement of business functions is not new; it predates ITIL. The idea of bringing the entire Service Management best practice together under one roof was, however, both radical and new.

Figure 1.1 shows each of the seven ITIL publications in relation to the framework.

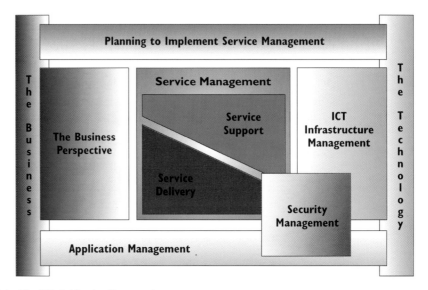

Figure 1.1 – The ITIL Publication Framework

1.4.1 Service Support

The *Service Support* book describes the five core support processes, which relate to the day-to-day support and maintenance of services to the user, together with the Service Desk function which provides a single point of contact and draws on all of the other processes. These five processes are:

- Incident Management
- Problem Management
- Change Management
- Configuration Management
- Release Management.

1.4.2 Service Delivery

The *Service Delivery* book describes all the five core delivery processes, which are more concerned with the future planning and improvement of IS service provision. These five processes are:

- Service Level Management
- Financial Management for IT Services
- Capacity Management
- Availability Management
- IT Service Continuity Management.

1.4.3 Planning to Implement Service Management

The *Planning to Implement Service Management* book examines the issues and tasks involved in planning, implementing and improving Service Management processes within an organisation, giving practical guidance in evaluating the current maturity levels of both the IS organisation and the Service Management processes involved. It also covers the issues associated with addressing cultural and organisational change, the development of a vision and strategy and the most appropriate method of approach.

1.4.4 ICT Infrastructure Management

The *Information Communications Technology (ICT) Infrastructure Management* book covers all aspects of technology infrastructure management from the identification of business requirements through the tendering process, to the testing, installation, deployment and subsequent ongoing support and maintenance of the ICT components and IS services. The book describes the major processes involved in the management of all areas and aspects of technology, covering all of the stages in the service life cycle and includes:

- Design and Planning
- Deployment
- Operations
- Technical Support.

1.4.5 Application Management

The book on *Application Management* addresses the complex subject of managing applications from the initial business requirements assessment, through the application life cycle, up to and including retirement. In addition, it covers the interaction with the Service Delivery, Service Support and ICT Infrastructure Management processes. The book places a strong emphasis on ensuring that IS projects and strategies are tightly aligned with those of the business throughout the applications life cycle, so as to ensure that the business obtains best value from its investment.

1.4.6 Security Management

The *Security Management* book details the process of planning and managing a defined level of security for information and IS services, including all aspects associated with Risk Management and reaction to security incidents. It also includes the assessment and management of risks and vulnerabilities, and the implementation of cost justifiable countermeasures.

1.4.7 The 'big picture' of ITIL processes

The seven core ITIL books together provide expansive coverage of all the elements necessary for the delivery of IS services within organisations, as depicted in Figure 1.2, which also captures the key interfaces between process areas.

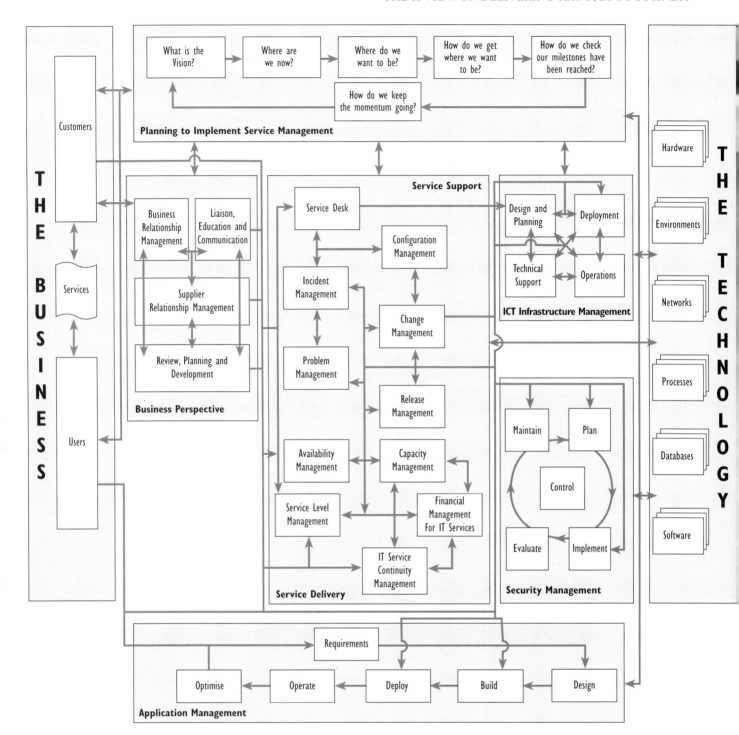

Figure 1.2 – The 'big picture' of ITIL processes and key interfaces

1.5   IS Management and Business Change guides

A further complimentary range of guides is also available from the OGC offering guidance on business changes issues, from setting direction, through organisational change to assessing performance, as well as guidance on acquiring and managing major services. These are aimed primarily at public sector readers, but useful to all.

1.5.1 How to Manage Business and IT Strategies

Creating a strategy and managing strategically are about making plans for your organisation that will achieve high-level goals while responding to an uncertain future.

This guide covers the reasons why strategic management is important, the process of creating a business strategy, how to manage strategically and ensure effective governance, and how to respond to change.

1.5.2 How to Manage Service Provision

Managing providers and services is all about achieving a realistic balance between what the business wants and what the provider can deliver while maintaining value for money.

This guide describes the main components of Service Management from a business point of view: managing service performance, the working relationship, the contract and changes to requirements.

1.5.3 How to Manage Service Acquisition

Acquiring services from private sector providers can bring economy, flexibility and innovation to public sector organisations, supporting the business and allowing a better focus on key activities. The process of acquiring services must be managed to ensure that services help the organisation achieve its strategic goals, and that value for money is obtained throughout the life of the contract.

This guide provides an overview of the process of acquiring a major service, from looking at strategic aims, through determining requirements, the formal procurement process and implementation, and recompetition at the end of a contract.

1.5.4 How to Manage Performance

This guide explains the principles of how to manage performance by determining critical business processes and creating a performance management framework to gauge their success.

It also covers setting targets, choosing good performance measures and analysing performance information, and includes useful techniques that will help you to achieve improvements in performance.

1.5.5 How to Manage Business Change

This guide explains how to manage the key components of business change – the organisation, its people and the external business environment.

It describes the process of managing business change, from the strategies behind it through to new ways of working and the realisation of benefits. It takes the reader step by step through the process of change and the questions and issues relevant at each stage. The approaches, techniques and questions it contains will be useful to any manager who is faced with the need for change – at any level and on any scale.

1.6 Reading guidance

This book has been structured to take the reader through a logical set of building blocks in understanding the Business Perspective approach to IT Service Management. This approach includes:

- a business focused cultural style to be adopted in the delivery of IS services
- a set of management processes focused on achieving business alignment
- effective management relationships and interfaces at strategic, tactical and operational levels.

Chapter 2 begins by addressing the key concepts which underpin the Business Perspective approach to IS service delivery. Included in this chapter are descriptions of some of the benefits, costs and problems associated with this approach.

Chapter 3 looks at the value of IT to the business, considering business value chains and how they can be used to understand the business value of IT.

Chapter 4 discusses business/IS alignment, including the management governance framework, setting IS directions and the three organisational levels of engagement: strategic, tactical and operational. However, at all times, it is key for IS to consider the perceptions and attitudes held by their customers and users working within the Business Units supported by the IS services, which is the theme for Chapter 5.

Having achieved an awareness of the business, its drivers, its needs and its perceptions, Chapters 6, 7 and 8 consider how these influence and impact the management of service provision, working with suppliers and the definition of roles and responsibilities.

Readers of this book should be aiming to 'adopt and adapt' the practices described in the book, on a scale appropriate to the size and complexity of their organisation, and the services and infrastructure to be managed. Whilst it is not essential that all aspects of this book be implemented, it is essential that all aspects are considered and evaluated with reference to the organisation and its requirements. Different elements of the book may be used and adapted in different ways to suit the individual requirements of each organisation.

2 CONCEPTS

The Business Perspective approach is achieved within IS by implementing a set of management processes and relationships throughout all areas, encouraging IS people to:

- consider the Business Perspective in all IS processes and activities
- have an understanding of the needs, impacts, drivers and requirements of the business through effective internal and external communication
- have effective and focused relationships with the business through the use of appropriate management
- consider themselves as an integral part of the business.

To be effective the processes should principally be aimed at aligning the business and IS. This alignment should not just consist of the current systems and services but also future systems and services. There is therefore a requirement to align all activities within all areas of IS, at all levels:

- **Strategic levels**: business strategies and IS strategies
- **Tactical levels**: business change programmes and IS change programmes
- **Operational levels**: business operational plans and IS operational plans.

When these activities are successfully aligned, the systems and services of the business and IS are aligned, and continue to be aligned. This alignment is an ongoing process and must continually be performed and reinforced by senior management both within the business and IS.

Within this book several key terms are used within a specific context. These terms are defined here with regard to their usage in this book and are repeated within the glossary contained in Appendix A, together with many other terms used within this book.

- **Business**: an overall **corporate** entity or organisation formed of a number of Business Units to provide a set of products or services, of which IS is one.
- **Business Customer**: a recipient of a product or a service provided by the organisation. For example if the organisation is a bank then this term is used to refer anyone using banking products or services.
- **Business Perspective**: this approach ensures that all IS activities are closely aligned with the business activities, and underpinned by a set of processes focused on achieving that alignment.
- **Business Unit**: a **segment** of the business entity by which both revenues are received and expenditure is caused or controlled, such revenues and expenditure being used to evaluate segmental performance. Usually IS is a separate Business Unit within the overall organisation.
- **Customer**: a recipient of a service; usually the customer has responsibility for **funding** the service, either directly through charging or indirectly in terms of demonstrable business need.
- **Information Communications Technologies (ICT)**: components (hardware, software, products etc.) necessary for the delivery of services to the users. It is the convergence of Information Technology, Telecommunications and Data Networking Technologies into a single integrated technology.

■ **Information Systems (IS)**: the overall organisation (unit/department/supplier) responsible for the support and management of the ICT infrastructure, including business applications, and for all aspects of the delivery and provision of services dependent upon that infrastructure.

■ **Service provider**: the unit responsible for the **provision** of IS services. The organisation supplying services or products to customers can be either internal to the organisation (IS department) or external (third party or outsource organisation).

■ **Supplier**: a third party responsible for **supplying** underpinning elements of the IS services. Suppliers may range from commodity hardware or software vendors, through network service providers and major hardware and software manufacturers, to major outsourcing organisations and strategic partnering relationships.

■ **User**: a person **using** services on a day-to-day basis, within the business.

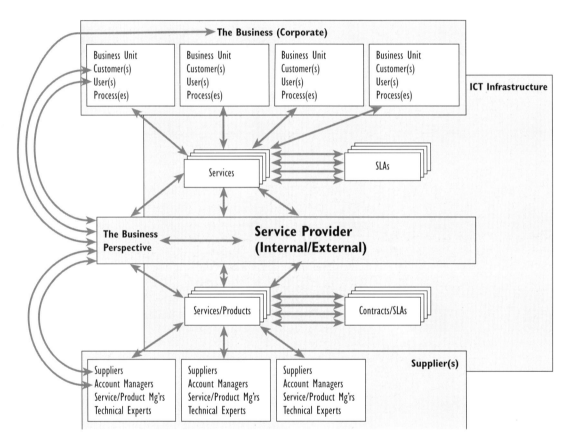

Figure 2.1 – The relationship model

The Business Perspective approach is built on the relationship model illustrated in Figure 2.1. A good Business Perspective is crucial to the establishment of good relationships between IS and the business and between IS and its suppliers. Managing relationships is the key activity of this approach, together with the provision of an effective communication channel between the various areas of the business, the service provider and the suppliers.

2.1 Goals, scope and objectives

The overall mission or goal of the Business Perspective approach is:

> **'To continually support and improve business effectiveness through the delivery of quality IS services aligned and responsive to business needs, while maximising the business return on investment in IS.'**

The overall scope of the Business Perspective approach can be defined in terms of:

> **'An approach to the establishment and ongoing management, of the relationships and interfaces at all levels, between the IS service provider and its customers and suppliers.'**

> **Tip**
>
> **The service provider has many relationships with many customers and managers, at many different levels within the business. It is essential therefore that all staff involved in IS activities are aware of their responsibility and accountability with regard to the Business Perspective approach and culture of IS, in support of the business.**

The principal objective of the Business Perspective approach is:

> **'To maintain and develop professional relationships with customers, suppliers and business managers at all levels which help identify business needs and opportunities to exploit existing and future IS capabilities for business benefit and advantage.'**

Other supporting objectives of this approach are to enable IS personnel to:

- understand how they contribute to business objectives
- deliver/improve IS services to underpin business objectives
- assist the business in maximising the exploitation of IS
- work with the business using the business management framework and business processes to run IS within the business
- enable a complementary and integrated culture with the business
- influence, innovate and enable change for business advantage.

2.2 The need

One of the biggest challenges facing senior business and IS managers is maintaining a continued alignment of IS services with business requirements. To achieve this, all capabilities within IS must be involved, including:

- people and culture – so that IS feel a part of the business
- processes – so that IS processes support business needs

- technology (the technology, products and tools) – to underpin IS and business processes
- suppliers, partners, manufacturers and vendors – so that they are focused on the needs of the business
- finance and the realisation of business benefit
- skills and knowledge.

The majority of this book deals with the processes involved within the Business Perspective approach although the roles, responsibilities, tools, deliverables and activities are also described.

Efficient IS organisations depend upon the integration, steering, direction and management of the four areas illustrated in Figure 2.2 – People, Processes, Technology and Suppliers. Suppliers, as shown within this diagram, is a term used to include suppliers, vendors, outsourcing organisations, partners and any other organisations that assist the service provider in the delivery of IS services to the business.

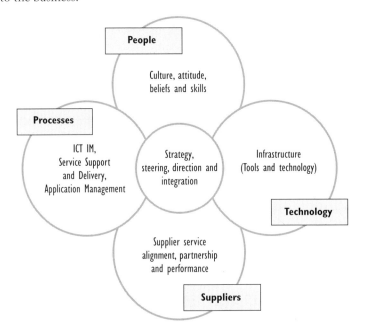

Figure 2.2 – People, Processes, Technology and Suppliers

The Business Perspective approach provides a focal point for the co-ordination of information between the business and IS. It provides a channel between all aspects of IS and the business for the receipt and distribution of business-related information. Success within an IS organisation depends on accurate, consistent and clearly focused interfaces being maintained with the business at all levels, as illustrated in Figure 2.3.

Information channels between IS and the business must act in both directions, in that the Business Perspective approach ensures that the views of the business are presented effectively to the service provider and the service provider's views are similarly presented to the business. These three levels of interface – strategic, tactical and operational – are dealt with in Chapter 4.

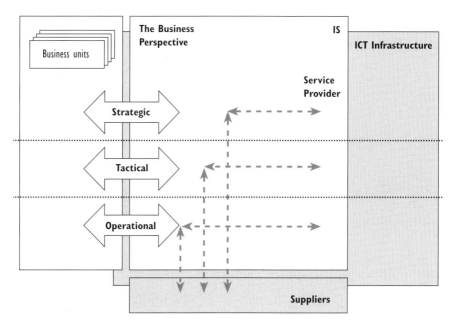

Figure 2.3 – The essential interfaces

2.3　Key process areas

There are four key process areas within the Business Perspective approach as illustrated in Figure 2.4 and outlined in Chapter 9:

- **Business Relationship Management**: involving the development of effective working relationships between the business and IS at strategic, tactical and operational levels. (This area is discussed in greater detail within Chapter 4.)

- **Supplier Relationship Management**: involving the development of effective working relationships between suppliers and IS at strategic, tactical and operational levels. (This area is discussed in greater detail within Chapter 7.)

- **Planning, Review and Development**: involving the continuous review and the planning of improvements within a business-focused culture in IS. This activity principally operates at the strategic level within IS. (This area is discussed in greater detail within Chapter 4.)

- **Liaison, Education and Communication**: involving the co-ordination and development of knowledge and skills, and the distribution of information relating to the Business Perspective within IS. These activities principally operate at the tactical and operational levels. (This area is discussed in greater detail within Chapter 6.)

It is essential that partnerships are forged between the business and IS, and IS and its suppliers, to ensure that a 'business-led' IS focus develops. This is especially true where functions or elements of the overall service are outsourced to these suppliers and they have a direct interface to and a direct impact upon the delivery of service to the customers and the business, as indicated by the dashed line in Figure 2.4. Staff working within this relationship area of IS are given many different roles, responsibilities and titles. Throughout this book IS personnel working within the business side of IS are referred to as Business Relationship Managers (BRMs) and those managing the supplier side are referred to as Supplier Relationship Managers (SRMs). In some smaller organisations a single person may undertake both the BRM and SRM roles, but for the sake of clarity within this book the functions are referred to individually and are illustrated as such in Figure 2.4 together with role descriptions in Chapter 8.

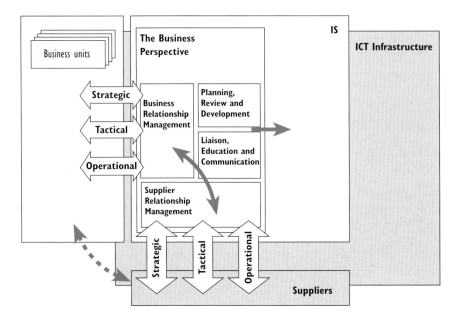

Figure 2.4 – Business Relationship Management and Supplier Relationship Management

It is essential that the two elements of Business Relationship Management and Supplier Relationship Management are co-ordinated to ensure that consistency of the culture and focus of all organisations and all personnel is maintained. The solid arrow in Figure 2.4 indicates this co-ordination as performed by the previously described Planning and Liaison processes.

Often to facilitate efficient working between IS and the business, 'user groups' are established to gather groups of people with similar objectives together. This enables information to be rapidly distributed and decisions to be made more quickly. One particular business and IS group is the IS or ICT Steering Group (ISG) which is crucial in maintaining alignment of the business and IS. This group is responsible for the investment, direction, focusing and prioritisation of IS activities.

As well as providing the alignment and communication channel between the business, IS and its suppliers, there is also a need to:

■ represent the business, customer and user view to all areas of IS and its suppliers and ensure consistency and accuracy of all business information

■ generate an increased understanding of the organisation's business throughout all areas of IS and its suppliers

■ evolve the service(s) to meet new and changing needs/demands of the business

■ develop a consistent overall culture that is business-aligned and business-focused at all levels within IS, developing the maturity of the IS organisation, as defined in the organisation growth model contained in the *Planning to Implement Service Management* book

■ measure the quality of IS service using targets that accurately represent the views and needs of the business

■ assist the business in the exploitation of current cost-effective technology

■ encourage and facilitate the introduction of innovative new IS solutions to meet specific business needs, where they are cost-effective and business sponsorship and approval have been obtained

- rapidly identify, develop and expand new IS opportunities within all areas of the business, where they add identifiable business benefits

- manage customer perception and expectation of what can be realistically achieved from IS investments with all the pitfalls and risks assessed.

It is also essential that business focus is maintained on developing and improving the quality of service delivered to the business by IS and that accountability for this is owned within IS. The Business Perspective approach provides that ownership with direction and focus, together with other Service Management processes, particularly the Service Level Management process (SLM).

All improvement initiatives are collated into an overall Service Improvement Programme (SIP), with the emphasis given to those activities that provide the greatest benefit to the business. This involves the calculation of a 'business realisation' value for each of the individual activities and the prioritisation of the activities based on this value. On completion of each activity a review is completed to determine whether each activity fully realised its anticipated business benefit.

| 2.4 | The role of IS in the business value chain |

If IS is to be truly aligned with the business it is essential that IS understands its role in the overall business value chain. The basic concept of generic value chains was first introduced by Michael Porter, Professor of Business Administration at Harvard University. In his book, *Competitive Advantage* (1998), Porter discusses the elements of the value chain in its component parts. We can align this model to an IS value chain easily and understand its relationships with the business by applying ITIL processes to the model. This technique is a key tool in the analysis of business dependence and strategic cost. It consists of identifying the main elements involved in the business process from the inbound logistics and the input of raw materials to the outbound logistics and retail of the end products or services to the organisation's customer. This concept is

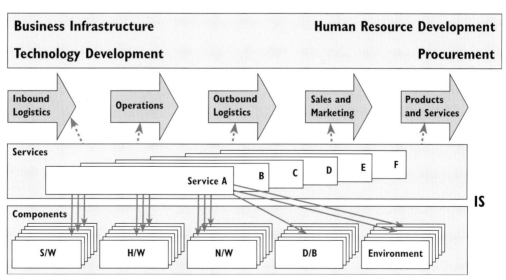

illustrated in Figure 2.5 and is explained in greater detail in Chapter 3.

Figure 2.5 – A typical value chain

Where value chain analysis techniques are used within the business, IS can also use the technique to analyse and understand the dependence of the business and business processes on the use of

IS systems and services. One of the requirements of the Business Perspective approach is to understand that dependence and to ensure that this is recognised and understood throughout IS. In addition this technique can also be used to identify the Vital Business Functions (VBFs) or critical business processes, the business-critical elements and their IS service dependence. These are key areas where the Business Perspective approach needs to work closely with the Service Level Management, Availability Management and IT Service Continuity Management processes, as described in the *Service Delivery* book.

However, it is not sufficient for IS just to continue to support the existing IS services and business processes. In the rapidly changing business world of today, IS, and specifically the Business-Perspective-driven processes within IS, should be producing innovative and creative plans and strategies that facilitate changes and even instigate changes within business processes by understanding business needs and processes.

IS should be proactively working with the business developing original solutions that stimulate improvements both in business and IS processes. This can only be achieved where business and IS planning processes are tightly aligned and integrated. However, these innovative solutions still need to be properly evaluated, managed and subjected to the usual feasibility study and business case procedures with sign off, prioritisation and approval from the business or at least the IS Steering Group (ISG) as discussed within the *ICT Infrastructure Management* book. Understanding the role of IS within the overall business value chain is one way of ensuring prioritisation is linked to business needs and benefit.

2.5 Exploiting IS and ICT for business advantage

The business environment is becoming increasingly driven to:

- increase stakeholder value
- increase shareholder value, delivering 'proven value for money'
- increase customer loyalty and retention
- improve corporate governance
- increase agility and improve the time to market
- increase market share and/or profit
- reduce overall costs.

All of these demands put increased pressure on organisations to become more and more effective. An efficient way of achieving this is better exploitation of ICT systems and IS services. This can be accomplished by developing improved relationships and communication mechanisms between the business, IS and its suppliers. The Business Perspective approach provides the focal point for the relationships and communication between all three areas. It is essential therefore that information is extracted from suppliers on the business advantages accruing from the use of new technology wherever and whenever possible. The benefits of adopting such technology in a rapid but structured manner are evaluated to extract the greatest business benefit from the implementation of innovative IS solutions and should only be considered where there is a business justification and benefit to be realised. By adopting this approach in a consistent way organisations gain the greatest overall benefit from the use of IS.

2.6 The business view

Business managers are responsible for the development, maintenance and continued operation of business processes. IS services are a component and in most cases one of the critical components of those business processes. The business needs IS services to operate just like any other service needed for the operation of its business processes, such as Human Resources or Facilities (accommodation, water, electricity, etc.). This means there is an expectation that the services are available and perform to the level required, when required, just like any other facility.

The business must get the availability, capacity, security, operability, recoverability and support they need as well as the required functionality. This means that IS staff need to be involved in the development and production of appropriate and relevant Service Level Requirements and Agreements (SLRs and SLAs) that detail the business quality targets, together with the required business functionality. All of the personnel working within these Business Perspective related areas need to interface with the Service Level Management process (SLM) to ensure that the targets contained within these SLRs and SLAs are an accurate representation of what the business agrees are their criteria for a quality service. However, it is equally important that all targets and timescales for both new and established services are achievable by the service provider. The expectation of the business, customers and users need to be carefully managed with regard to all of these areas. This appreciation of the business viewpoint is considered in greater depth in Chapter 5.

From the business view it is essential that IS and the services provided are perceived to be:

- delivering business value
- easy to use and communicate with
- responsive and courteous
- available when required
- consistent and perform to quality criteria and targets
- aware of and aligned to the business needs and processes
- proactive, wherever possible.

The Business Perspective approach should also ensure that the business understands its own responsibilities in the above areas and that it respects the limitations and budgetary constraints that are imposed upon IS and its operation.

Frequently individual managers within the business specialise in dealing with and managing the business/IS interface. These are often referred to as Informed Customers (ICs). The use of ICs often encourages the business to develop closer relationships with IS and develop specialised IS knowledge and skills within particular business areas and units. This role is discussed in Chapter 5.

The interface between IS, business managers and ICs is critical to the success of IS and is frequently not given the necessary focus and resource. There are many ways of improving this interface. Two of the most successful ways are to use focused, active service reports and Portfolio Management. Portfolio Management requires the development and maintenance of a 'Portfolio of Services'. This is an extension of the Service Catalogue and is often amalgamated into one set of combined information. Portfolio Management involves using information relating to all of the existing live services, development services and proposed new services to market IS to all areas of the business, thus exploiting the use of IS services within the business for maximum business benefit. This aspect is covered more fully in Section 5.3.

2.7   The provider's view

The service provider is responsible for providing IS services and must focus on the provision of cost-effective, quality services aligned to business needs. To achieve this they must work closely with their customers and business managers in the definition, agreement and measurement of quality targets aligned to the expectation of the business. These targets should be jointly agreed and documented within SLRs and SLAs and measured and reported on within service reports. In this way the expectations of both IS and the business are aligned with common goals.

Another method of maintaining good focus is to use the Balanced Scorecard (BSC) approach to align business and IS objectives and targets. IS objectives are aligned to those within the appropriate Business Units and to overall corporate objectives. Critical Success Factors (CSFs) and Key Performance Indicators (KPIs) are established to measure the success in meeting these objectives. Use of the BSC is discussed in Chapter 4.

The service provider is invariably controlled by finite budgets and expenditure and must therefore focus on what can and cannot be achieved within the current budget allocations. One of the most demanding challenges for IS is the balancing of conflicting demands of specific Business Units with corporate initiatives and corporate change programmes, or the often conflicting demands of individual Business Units. All decisions within this area must therefore be made by the Board or the ISG and not made arbitrarily by IS in isolation. It is also vital that the business perceives IS as an effective investment and a 'value for money' service rather than as an 'expensive overhead' or a 'waste of money'.

Some of the best service providers go further than just the development and implementation of business focused SLAs and services. These organisations develop a culture throughout IS where everyone is focused on:

- the needs of the business, the business processes and business value chains
- the needs and desires of the customers
- the delivery of quality services
- the implementation of efficient, best practice processes
- the exploitation of technology for business benefit and advantage
- a philosophy of continuous improvement
- knowing and understanding the business and its mission statement
- cost efficiency and delivering value.

One way for an organisation to achieve this is to adopt the 'Moment of Truth' philosophy of Carlsson.

> **Tip**
>
> *Moments of Truth*
>
> **The CEO of Scandinavian Airlines, Jan Carlsson, developed this concept in the 1980s. Each interaction between the service provider and their customer is defined as a 'Moment of Truth'. Everyone within the provider organisation is tasked with understanding the customer point of view, simplifying the customer interface and trying to improve the quality of the customer experience.**

This technique involves identifying each customer interaction with the IS service provider and then implementing cost-justifiable activities to make each encounter as simple, easy, enjoyable and as efficient as possible. This technique is further explored in Chapter 4.

The service provider should be committed to the continued development and improvement of effective, business-driven, ITIL best practice processes. The Business Perspective approach enables all areas of IS to focus on those areas of greatest business need, benefit and impact, thus directing all areas of IS activity as described in Chapter 6.

In the most forward-looking organisations the ITIL processes are not exclusive to IS. These processes are equally applicable to the business itself. In fact, in many organisations the business has contracts and agreements with its own Business Customers and has Service Level Managers, Service Delivery Managers, Customer Managers, Customer Service Managers and Client Managers, managing those relationships and agreements. This is obviously a business-owned process. It is fundamental to the successful operation of the business that both the business and IS processes are 'joined up' and that the targets they contain are consistent. The Business Perspective approach helps ensure the consistency, alignment and integration of the business and IS processes and targets by establishing consistency and integration between the business SLM and the IS SLM roles and processes. This is achieved when the IS SLM process becomes a constituent part of a wider business SLM process and role. This principle is equally applicable to all of the ITIL processes and they function far more effectively when they operate as a fully integrated component of a business-owned process. This is especially true of the Change Management, Capacity Management and IT Service Continuity Management processes. This is illustrated for Change Management in Figure 2.6.

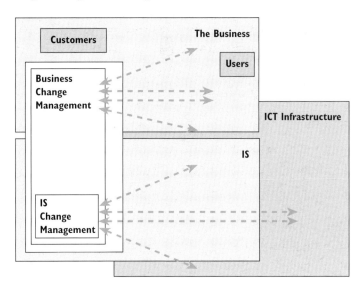

Figure 2.6 – Business-owned ITIL processes

2.8   The supplier's view

The main drivers for IS suppliers are to achieve stakeholder satisfaction and make a long-term sustainable profit from the relationship with the service provider, while achieving the satisfaction of both the IS functions they support and business served by IS. However, if the relationship is to be successful for both sides then there has to be a certain empathy between the cultures of the organisations involved. The supplier not only has 'Moments of Truth' with the IS service provider of the organisation, but almost invariably has them with the customers, users and business managers.

The contract and adherence to the contract with the supplier is crucial to a successful working relationship between the supplier, the IS service provider and the Business Units of the organisation. Therefore the targets contained within the contract must underpin the targets contained within the SLAs. The focus for the supplier must be on meeting or if possible exceeding all of the targets and requirements within the contract and any attached schedule. However, the supplier must also address the softer issues, including the cultural aspects, and ensure that all of their staff involved within the contract are focused on the business and customer requirements and the delivery of quality services.

The aim of the supplier should be similar to that of the service provider, and that is to develop a relationship with both the IS service provider unit and the Business Units so that all organisations are aligned and consistent at all levels. The supplier should, like the IS service provider, be committed to the continued development and improvement of effective, business-driven, ITIL best practice processes. Ideally the service provider and the supplier have common terminology and codes of management, and Service Management practice based on ITIL. This allows the processes of each of the organisations to be business-driven and closely integrated, as described in Chapter 7. In the case of an outsourced organisation, where they are the IS service provider, the relationship with the business is a more direct one and is critical to the success of the continued relationship.

2.9   Business change

Business managers need to recognise the criticality of IS to their business processes and to adequately provide for the management of both the business process and the underpinning IS services. For example many Business Unit managers fail to recognise the fact that services such as email have become critical to most organisations and that it is frequently used to drive internal business processes. Changes in business direction, processes, products, services and/or operational activity generally have an impact on the supporting IS elements. In managing such change it is imperative that the business dependence on IS is adequately assessed and reassessed, to ensure that both the business and IS understand the risks, implications, benefits and the potential impacts of the proposed changes.

In spite of the investment of time in aligning business and IS strategy, it is still very difficult to predict changes in business direction, market direction, industry direction or radical changes in business needs. All of these can have significant and dramatic impact on the service provider. Therefore resilient and adaptable strategies that can rapidly accommodate changes are essential, particularly to the service provider.

Personnel working within relationship activities are likely to be involved in the early stages and discussions of all new business requirements for all new services or major modifications to existing services. The relationship and scope of corporate programme/change management and IS Change Management processes need to be clearly defined to ensure that the requirements of Change Management are raised appropriately. Some organisations consider the capture of an idea or potential development by BRMs as the first stage of the change life cycle. The BRMs can be of major benefit to Change Management as they can act as the initial filter for the sponsorship of business changes. This ensures that the change is desirable, that sufficient budget exists to support the change and that the request is co-ordinated with the other requests raised from the same or other business areas.

An effective Business Perspective approach throughout IS ensures that all projects and changes are driven and scheduled according to business impact and urgency. In leading organisations the change process is a process owned and managed by the business, and IS is an integral yet essential subsidiary element.

2.10 Benefits, costs and possible problems

When considering a Business Perspective approach within an organisation the specific benefits, costs and possible problems should be identified and quantified. Some generic benefits, costs and possible problems associated with this approach have been identified and are detailed in the following sections.

2.10.1 Benefits

The number of IS service providers recognising the generic benefits that can be accrued from adopting ITIL best practice are rapidly increasing. From the business viewpoint, the adoption of ITIL processes by IS service providers is likely to manifest itself through service quality improvements, and the importance of specific benefits varies between organisations. Typical direct benefits that an organisation can expect from the adoption of a more active use of a Business Perspective approach are realised in two areas: business and IS.

Benefits to the business

The benefits to the business associated with an effective Business Perspective approach are:

- more appropriate funding and targeting of investment in IS, based on business need:
  - maximised return on IS investment and the cost-effective provision of IS services together with more efficient use of IS resources, leading to a reduced Total Cost of Ownership (TCO) and long-term reduction of costs or an increased investment in new initiatives or business projects
  - improved use of suppliers with more effective negotiation of better contractual terms and using supplier's economies of scale
- improved quality of IS service:
  - improved quality of service to the business, with IS processes that truly underpin and align with business processes, leading to improved business productivity and revenue
  - projects more likely to satisfy customer needs
- improved relationships and communication with IS:
  - consistent and more business-focused IS service delivery, where IS services and their delivery are more closely aligned to business requirements, priorities and impacts (e.g. incidents, problems and changes) because of improved communication and information flows

- planned IS purchase, development and implementation more aligned to business priorities using Portfolio Management techniques
- better business focus and management information on IS processes and services
- improved working relationships with IS and its suppliers, through better interfaces and contacts

■ improved business operation:
- improved 'time to market' for new business products and services, from a more responsive IS unit, with improved definition of business requirements
- projects and changes implemented to agreed quality and targets, which more accurately reflect business impacts and urgencies
- faster and improved quality of IS support and response to business needs by more rapid and accurate identification of business requirements
- IS service continuity and recovery more aligned to business impact, urgency and need
- business needs accurately and speedily reflected into the IS environment
- co-ordinated changing business needs with an evolving IS environment.

Benefits to IS

The benefits to IS from the adoption of a Business Perspective approach are:

■ improved relationships and communication with the business:
- improved working relationships with the business, with an improved flow of information from the business, leading to better forecasting and alignment of IS requirements
- business expectation more in line with IS capability, with SLR, SLA, OLA, project, change and contract targets better aligned with business requirements, more realistic and achievable

■ improved efficiency and effectiveness of IS providing stability with an improved long-term future, greater customer satisfaction and retention:
- increased IS customer and business satisfaction and retention because IS services are better value for money and more closely aligned to business requirements, through improved implementation of major changes and better use and management of suppliers and contracts
- improved reputation for IS through increased levels of customer service

■ improved culture and attitude within IS, because of improved business knowledge and awareness:
- increased effectiveness of key IS personnel, with more efficient use of resources, leading to improved classification of incidents and therefore reduced incident and problem resolution times
- reduced risk of failure in meeting business commitments
- greater levels of IS staff satisfaction

■ greater professionalism of IS delivering improved quality of service:
- earlier identification and warning of business-critical situations
- more proactive development and improvement of technology and services by faster exploitation of appropriate technology, driven by business needs

- ability to handle higher volumes of business projects and changes with better management, co-ordination and reduced adverse impact on the delivery of IS services
- better and more informed planning and acquisition of ICT components and services, plus services and systems that are not over-engineered, but are designed to meet achievable business and operational targets and timescales

- improved relationships and communication with suppliers:
  - better management of suppliers with improved supplier performance to contractual targets more aligned to business and IS needs
  - improved value for money from suppliers and contracts freeing resources for investment in other areas
  - access to specialist expertise and knowledge that are not cost-effective to retain in house
  - access to an external view and identification of possible additional areas of improvement for the service provider from suppliers with expertise in a variety of different environments.

2.10.2 Costs

The costs associated with an effective and efficient Business Perspective approach within IS are:

- increased need for proactive management time and planning resources
- customer surveys and marketing campaigns
- communication strategies, publication, deployment and training
- staff recruitment, development, training and the possible use of external consultants
- development of processes, procedures and documentation
- procurement of additional tools, hardware and software
- implementation of cultural change programmes.

2.10.3 Possible problems

Some of the principal problems that may be associated with the implementation or improvement of a Business Perspective approach within IS are:

- lack of management commitment and support
- use of inappropriate staff in customer, business and strategic positions
- Business Relationship Management and Supplier Relationship Management staff being drawn into reactive roles and not being allowed to devote time to develop proactive activities
- over-expectation that the Business Perspective approach will deliver benefits quickly; however, relationships and strategic issues take time to deliver value
- lack of willingness and commitment from both the business and IS to make the relationship work
- incorrect positioning of the role within the organisation causing failure of the process to operate at the correct level
- inefficient use of resources causing wasted spend and investment or inadequate resources, budget and time

- lack of willingness in the business and/or suppliers to work closely with the Business Perspective processes
- lack of corporate objectives, strategies, policies, and business direction
- lack of knowledge and appreciation of business impacts and priorities
- resistance to change and cultural change
- poor relationships, communication and a lack of co-operation between IS and the business
- IS dictating to the business, or the business dictating to IS; it must be a balanced partnership to succeed, with the business leading the partnership
- lack of training or inadequate management of the succession cycle in the replacement of staff
- continued unrealistic business perceptions and expectations with a low success rate in IS delivery
- lack of tools, standards and skills, or tools too complex and costly to implement and maintain
- lack of information, monitoring and measurements or demonstrable performance metrics
- unreasonable targets and timescales, e.g. service targets, SLAs and OLAs
- poor supplier management and/or poor supplier performance
- lack of customer and business awareness and cost consciousness within IS.

3 THE VALUE OF IT

Much has been written in the IT industry about the value that IT contributes to businesses. The impression within IS is that the business always benefits from increased and/or more sophisticated IS provision. However, to place proper context around what is meant by value, the circumstances in which IS delivers real and usable value to the business must be understood. Understanding the Business Perspective of IT value is a revealing look at far more than just what things cost. Value is often equated in monetary terms, and while this is partly a measure of value, it isn't the entire picture especially when IS is judged by its cost, without due regard for its contribution. Additionally, factors other than costs and revenue can be significant measures of value. This can be the case, especially in public sector organisations, where the ability to comply with government requirements can exceed cost considerations. One good measure of value is the reciprocal opportunities that result from proper alignment between the business and IS. This recognises the need for two-way generation and mutual development of contribution, as illustrated through the business's expression of requirements and IS suggestions on technical (or procedural) changes which offer meaningful value to the business.

3.1 Business value chain

The IT industry has long thought of itself, often simplistically, as an enabler simply because it is there and it is used, without any attempt to understand how the value is delivered and perceived. Without that understanding of the value from a Business Perspective, it is not possible to maximise delivered value within the available resources and constraints. The differences in perceptions must be understood and translated into a common understanding, which can then lead to mutually supported improvement initiatives. This chapter provides an approach which enables both IS and the business to see themselves in the value chain.

It is the way that technology (including ICT) is applied by the business that adds value. The application of the technology tends to be under the control of business managers and users rather than the engineers who developed it or those who provide supporting services.

The sophistication of the technology is not necessarily related to the value added – the technology may vary from a pencil to a fully automated production line. In each case the value can, and should, be determined and understood in terms of how the business benefits from the development, implementation and support of that technology – i.e. why is the business better off? Because it is in a better place compared to where it would be without that technology.

3.2 Understanding the business value chain

To understand, demonstrate and justify the business value of IT we need to understand the business value chain and where IS adds, or could add, value.

Michael Porter introduced the 'value chain' concept in 1985 in his book *Competitive Advantage* (1998). The idea was simply presented: that we need to know how the activities of a business add value to the business and how the activities relate to one another in providing overall value.

He identified that the day-to-day operational and support processes added value when they all worked well together. The value was from the linkages creating end-to-end process capabilities. He identified the 'primary' process capabilities that linked horizontally across the enterprise, as shown in Figure 3.1.

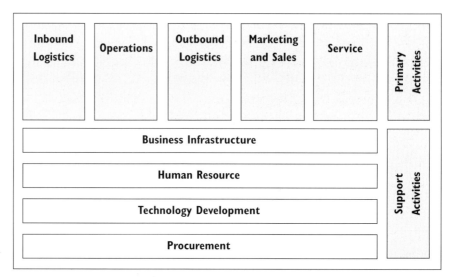

Figure 3.1 – Porter's primary value chain

He also identified that there were other processes within an organisation's Infrastructure, Human Resource, Technology Development and Procurement which were 'support' capabilities and that these capabilities linked horizontally across the supply chain.

Today Porter's value chain is updated with 'People, Process, Technology and Suppliers' to replace Infrastructure, Human Resource, Technology Development and Procurement. These are the capabilities that enable the primary processes of delivery of products and services to markets and customers to be undertaken effectively, as illustrated in Figure 3.2.

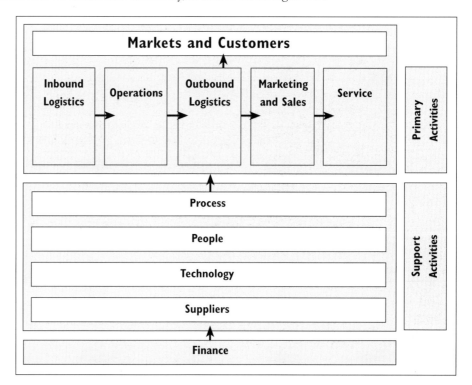

Figure 3.2 – Porter's total value chain

Figure 3.2 shows Finance underpinning the value chain where money is invested in the business's capabilities to deliver value back to the organisation, as shown through bottom-line profit.

> **Tip**
>
> **In terms of 'value chain', relevant contributions at any stage of the chain result in an identifiable benefit to the end product, i.e. the output from the chain.**

IS tend to view the business value chain as comprising the underlying technologies that customers use in their daily operations (which contribute to the end product or service offered by the business to its customers) and the framework of services that manage the ICT infrastructure. IS understands the IS part of the chain and how the technology components fit together, but traditionally is not likely to have a working comprehension of how those technology elements fit into the overall value chain of the organisation's business processes.

3.2.1   The customer view

Most business people don't think of IS in value terms, they think in cost terms. IS budget, IS spending, Total Cost of Ownership (TCO) … these are the concepts typically associated with IS and explored in Section 4.7, Financial Management.

The business concerns itself with bottom-line profit, repeat customer business, the evolution of market space and product innovation. IS is seen as one ingredient to the end result, in and of itself not deserving of recognition as an entity on its own. IS is an integral, but peripheral part of a business value chain. While public sector and not-for-profit organisations are not driven by bottom-line profits, they are none the less driven by delivering a product, usually a service to their customers. Similar to their counterparts in profit-driven companies, they see IS as an ingredient to the overall business deliverables.

> **Tip**
>
> **The customer sees the value chain in their terms. Ask a businessperson what value he or she brings to the organisation. A Sales Manager might tell you how much their territory produces in monetary value. A Division Head might tell you how much revenue or profit the unit brings in each year. These individuals measure IS using their perspectives. For IS to demonstrate its contribution, it must do so in terms that each of these disparate customer areas can relate to and ensure IS aligns with the goals and objectives of the whole organisation.**

3.2.2   The business/IS-aligned view

The alignment between the IS view and the customer view gains value when IS is able to identify the relationship between the technologies and the business processes they support. This can be accomplished by understanding and articulating IS services in business terms. Each contributor to the value chain, including the customer, IS and external suppliers needs to understand IS services within the same business context to create a true consolidated view of IS value.

Over the last 30 years most businesses have not developed the People, Process and Technology capabilities together or in balance. These three capabilities have been developed under different governance arrangements. IS has typically been subject to the full rigours of Project Management, whilst People and Process management has been left to line management to plan and develop. Heavy investments in IS thinking and IS development have not been matched with investments in Process thinking and Process development.

This matching of investment time and effort in People, Process and Technology has been the biggest problem experienced in most organisations in deploying and exploiting technology-based business developments.

Value chains are only effective if they are aligned and balanced – if People, Process and Technology capabilities are designed to work together in concert. Planning and development of Technology needs to be matched with the planning and development of the business's People and Processes to get the value from the Technology investment.

3.2.3   IT value in service quality

If unreliable services are provided, value is lost. If IS is unresponsive to issues, providing periods when services are unavailable, slow or insecure, the lack of service quality contributes to the lack of perceived IS value by the business. In other words – would the business be better the way it previously operated, rather than the way it operates now with IS service imperfections? Ask a customer who has lost the competitive advantage to be first to market with a new product and you don't have to guess at the answer!

We all know that the quality of service is relative – many people accept poor service just to get the right product. We also know that in competitive situations, if you cannot get the service right, then people look elsewhere. It is a matter of balance and trade-offs. This is especially true today, where outsourcing of IS services is an option, and business interest in considering this in the pursuit of IT value is increasing. IS cannot afford to underestimate the quality of IS services as a key ingredient to overall IT value. As such the consideration of not only providing the 'IT' but in a consistent, measurable and sustainable way is as important as the People, Process and Technology are themselves.

3.2.4   IT value in managing service cost

What are the IS costs that we are concerned about?

In this case we are looking at the total costs of IS, the Total Cost of Ownership which means the cost of the life cycle of developing, providing and sustaining IS services.

Is it acceptable to be cost-conscious with day-to-day operational and support costs but to allow an element of extravagance with development and deployment costs?

In many IS departments there have been two conflicting worlds:

- the development world where money is not the issue – so desperate have IS and business management been that development is frequently achieved or failed without due regard for cost
- the operational and support world where costs are continually under constraints.

There needs to be a business benefit driven approach to investment and funding, based on meeting the business requirements now and in the future, and optimising the return on that investment.

3.2.5 The supplier value chain

Chapter 7 on Supplier Relationship Management deals with the processes around managing suppliers. The point made in this chapter is that suppliers, like business internal functions, add value. The value can be seen as a product or a service. However, if that product or service is integrated with the products, services and capabilities of the customer, the value added is through the integration of value chains.

The more tightly and effectively a supplier's products, services and capabilities are integrated the more value the supplier provides.

If we look at a supplier's technology for delivering its services, the better the technology interfaces with that of the customer, the smoother the working relationship. If we look at a supplier's processes, the more compatible they are with the customer, again the more smoothly the businesses run.

Figure 3.3 illustrates the supplier value chains in the context of the business.

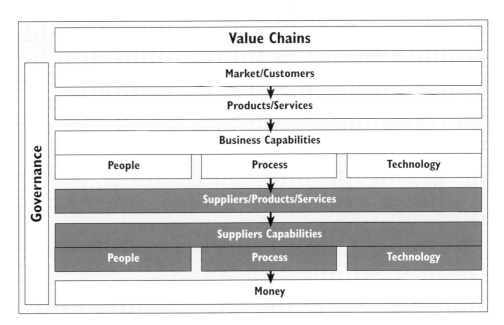

Figure 3.3 – The supply chain – value chain

Supplier Relationship Management is one area where shared standards regarding process and technology add value to both sides of the relationship. The process standards that ITIL provides along with Service Management tools enable IS functions to work more closely with one or a number of suppliers.

3.3   IT value to business development

IS is capable of providing value through stability of service provision to 'business as usual' and where change brings associated risks, to both the Business and IS, these need to be managed to ensure appropriate levels of stability. However, the value of IT is also in being responsive to change and new challenges.

IS needs to be able to support business development and growth in a number of ways: its entry into new markets, capture of new customers, radical development of new products and business services. IS can help in business acquisition and rationalisation, in the rapid deployment of IS into newly acquired business and in support of major business consolidation initiatives. On the negative side, failure of IS to be involved can be detrimental to acquisition and merger activities.

Example

An initial attempt at a merger between two financial organisations was initiated. The merger was announced publicly and then embarrassingly called off months later when IS support for the two organisations turned out to be irreconcilable. The merger finally happened many years later, with ultimate success based on lessons learned from bitter experience, and upon acceptance of compromises from all quarters, based upon a broader understanding of requirements on both sides.

3.4 Establishing a value culture

'In the past, man was first. In the future the system will be first.' (Frederick Winslow Taylor)

In 1911, Frederick Winslow Taylor wrote about scientific management and systemising efficiency. Unfortunately, Taylor's system turned the worker into a disposable human tool, a worker-for-hire, a wage serf, as satirised in the classic movie *Modern Times*, where Charlie Chaplin becomes a mere cog in the assembly line. Taylor's system dehumanised the worker and the culture of work, pitting workers against technology.

Taylor was also oblivious to another danger inherent in his system: it left ownership, control and the distribution of profits in the hands of a small elite group of managers, time-study engineers and owners. His system offered once self-reliant workers higher wages in exchange for their loyalty to what many consider a modern form of feudalism.

Most companies today still operate within a top-down vision of the workplace. However, because of global and technological change, companies are recognising that their survival and success requires changes in the way they 'do business'. More and more, they are seeking new, more flexible ways of rewarding and motivating their workers whilst controlling costs and delivering ever-higher levels of value to their customers. They are also realising that these objectives are impeded by the adversarial nature of the surrounding economic and cultural environment, a by-product of Taylor's philosophy of work and the inherent instability of the wage system. Businesses are coming to see that what is needed is a new way of thinking.

So far, we have discussed the value chain philosophy from the vantage point of IS understanding a Business Perspective of value. An important ingredient to instil in a value culture is also the understanding of the value chain within the IS organisation itself. The concept is no different here, except that the internal adoption of a value culture sets the context for IS staff to then apply the value chain outwardly into the business. Many IS organisations have done this to emphasise the dependencies of a value chain and practise these through lateral teams of value-chain activities.

Establishing a value culture means providing a style of leadership that nurtures autonomy, ownership and a sense of value for the service delivered to the customer. This begins at the highest levels in the IS organisation, but is evolved, sustained, improved and practiced at the grass roots level. From this perspective, IS staff become the customer. As customers they experience quality, satisfaction, value, loyalty and growth. The best leadership styles – those that demonstrate and practise a customer-centric value system – can propel IS organisations farther and faster. However, the grass roots need to be groomed well and selected for their roles for a mature cultural change to take hold.

Nurturing a value culture within IS can begin by taking a horizontal view of the IS organisation. The customer is a part of this view as the business sponsor and supporter of the IS organisation.

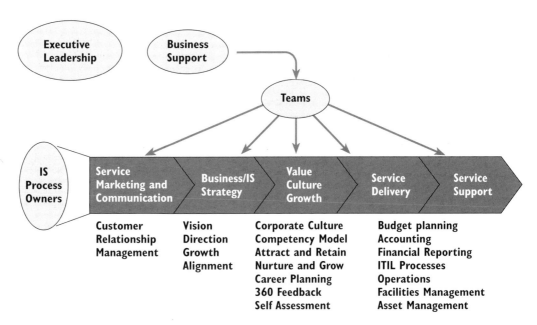

Figure 3.4 – The structure of a horizontal IS organisation

Figure 3.4 is an example of what the structure of a horizontal IS organisation might resemble. The organisation is championed by executive leadership both from IS and the Business. IS core areas within the horizontal structure form a multi-disciplinary team and provide inputs to each area within the core. Each core has a process owner to set targets and deliverables for that area. The area deliverables are underpinned by process activities that support the deliverable and every member of the team has a responsibility to contribute.

Figure 3.5 shows the flow, the evolution of requirements and subsequent delivery of services, and of the required added value at each step. The key concept of the value chain is that each element needs the contribution of those responsible for that element if the chain as a whole is to function and deliver value to the business – by which it will be judged. For this chain to work, it needs to be more than one person or group receiving input, doing their part and then passing it on. Understanding the whole chain and the inputs and outputs to one's own element of the chain is central to successful delivery of the final service, and perhaps even more importantly, to maintenance of the value chain.

Figure 3.5 – The value chain flow

Example

For the development of an IS service that delivers business benefit, such as laser scanning at supermarket checkouts:

■ the need for a business advantage appealing to customers is recognised

■ possibilities and options are discussed within the team, which includes IS who suggest technological advances which might make new ideas, not previously possible, now possible

■ the requirements of the stores are determined and the necessary hardware, software, etc. for the solution are determined and developed

■ the solution is tested and implemented and IS staff brought up to the level of expertise required to implement and support it

■ the new service is implemented and taken into normal service and staff support it as part of normal operation.

The strength of the chain analogy is that staff communicate as functional understanding and 'hand-over' requires, without all communication going back through multiple levels of management.

The characteristics of the integrated view include those of process value ownership:

■ no traditional hierarchy or silos of reporting or accountability

■ focus is on core value processes – our main thing

■ multi-discipline and cross-team activities form the core

■ process owners define the deliverables

■ each core process maps to a Balanced Scorecard (see Chapter 4 for more information on Balanced Scorecard).

3.5   Value chains and business governance

Governance aligns the strategy, planning, development, operation and support of People, Process and Technology capabilities along with the strategy, planning, development, operation and support of products, services, markets and customers.

Common governance enables the business value chains to be aligned so that they all get planned, developed, operated and supported in a common management manner by the business. The governance framework is further discussed in Section 4.3.

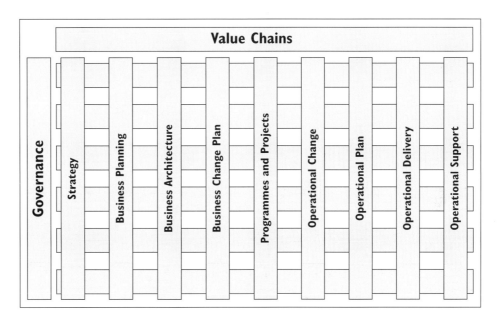

Figure 3.6 – The governance framework and value chains

In Figure 3.6 the vertical bars (reading from left to right) represent the governance processes as they evolve from strategic vision to operational execution.

3.6   Demonstrating and exploiting value chains

The linkages between the business and IS offer opportunities to exploit and improve the overall cost position of the business, e.g. only when the role of the service provider is fully understood can it be expanded to the benefit of all parties.

> **Example**
>
> In the provision of logistics services, logistics suppliers are extending their services into areas traditionally occupied by the production process, initiated by recognising processes rather than physical location. Simply illustrated, large global manufacturing companies have entrusted external suppliers, specialising in supply chain management solutions, with full ownership of the logistics chain, delivering to the final point of use at the production line.

Key success factors for achieving this include:

- share appropriate value activities – identify value activity linkages and assess the benefit of sharing
- knowledge transfer of value activity management – this does not generally occur naturally, the business and IS need to develop strategies to execute knowledge transfer to identify, reinforce and extend knowledge within the value chain.

3.7 Valuing IS

Time to market is one of the critical ingredients in a successful business venture. All the planning, marketing, infrastructure and intelligence is lost, if new business is usurped by another company who does it first, not necessarily better. The consuming public doesn't care initially, 'new' is the draw, not quality. Traditionally IS have often been the cause of delays and consequential losses, and even company bankruptcies.

Example

A very successful 'mail order' company realised that their order processing and control systems were being outgrown by their sales expansions and diversifications. A new system was commissioned and ordered, but the IS supplier was late in delivery. Instead of the system being ready before the spring peak of orders, it was not in place until the autumn. When installed, the system fully met requirements and greatly improved order turn-around time, delivering a better service to customers. However, by then too many customers had failed to receive their orders when they needed them – many orders were cancelled and many customers did not use that company again. Within nine months they had been driven into significant loss, and were purchased by a competitor who made use only of their trading name. The new IS services were discontinued.

IS and the business must be mutually involved in the continuous measurement of value, balance and planning to understand fully the expectations for growth, market shift and technological exploitation opportunities, to be fully aligned and prepared to meet consumer demand.

Applying a Business Perspective through the recognition, use and continuous improvement of IS service is achievable, but only with a clear understanding of IS value both within IS and the business. There must be a common vision among all in the service value chain and, most of all, a continuous commitment to improve, measure and improve again. One of the key messages here is that IS value must be understood throughout the supply and value chain (singular of chain here is deliberate). Only if the key areas of IS share the same values as the business will the outcome be successful.

Although the IT industry had traditionally employed a variety of methods and techniques to place a quantitative value on IT, there has been a tendency to concentrate on internal metrics that describe only how IS is doing in its own terms, e.g. in terms of incidents, changes, capacity and performance. More usefully, in terms of delivering services from a Business Perspective, the quantitative values need to reflect the extent to which the IS services support the business, e.g. customer satisfaction, production figures, accuracy of invoices. The quantitative values provide benchmarks and comparisons over time that indicate how IS value is performing. Chapter 4 further discusses benchmarking and depicts ways to measure IS value in terms of a Return on Investment in IS activities from a Business Perspective.

4 THE APPROACH TO BUSINESS/IS ALIGNMENT

Tip

Service providers need to know and understand the business environment, drivers and the customers. It is also vitally important that the customers and users of the IS services understand the IS environment, its capabilities and the IS service providers.

Is the alignment of IS with the business an issue? Those who say 'Yes' are in the company of many businesses and IS functions that share this concern. From the business point of view, IS is remote, something which is 'over there'. From the IS point of view, business seems to be impenetrable. The problems are real and, for many, long-standing. For many businesses the problems end up in divorce with wholesale outsourcing of the IS function.

The two questions to ask at this point are:

- ■ Whose problem is it?
- ■ What needs to be taken into account in addressing the problem?

The first question is explored below and the second question in the remainder of this chapter.

4.1 Whose problem is it?

4.1.1 Does the alignment problem belong to IS?

Is the alignment problem the fault of IS and for IS to resolve? Is the alignment problem one of culture – with technical experts appearing to rule the roost? Is the problem to do with the mystique that IS has built up over years of almost assumed superiority? Is it of language where IS has so many terms and so much complexity that the business is left distanced? Is the problem a lack of shared vision and drivers and goals? Is it the problem one of remoteness where few IS people have seen the business front line and have certainly never worked on the front line dealing with Business Customers?

The problem of alignments is all of these and, what is worse, the problem is almost unique to IS.

Do other primary or support functions have the same problem – do sales, production or finance have problems aligning with the business? The answer is clearly 'No' – despite the fact that the cultures of sales and production, for example, are very different.

It is bizarre if IS is not aligned with the business because IS has helped all the business functions align with each other. IS has provided best-of-breed solutions and integrated Enterprise Resource Planning (ERP) solutions that align the business functions. IS has enabled wholesale implementation of Business Process Models.

Yet IS has not used IS to align itself with the business. IS has acquired its own tools for scheduling and support despite the fact that many businesses have business tools and systems for scheduling and supporting production and service. IS has enabled a high level of business process integration with ERP solutions yet there are no ERP solutions for IS itself. Nor does IS have its own integrated Process Model – just lots of poorly connected flowcharts.

It is even worse than this. IS is not aligned with the business but neither is IS aligned with itself. The best-of-breed ERP for IS are sets of unrelated tools. Professional service automation tools for service development and Service Management tools for service delivery work in separate parts of IS, with little or no recognition of each other in terms of shared or interfacing process or data.

Many IS practitioners regard themselves as just that, and take no interest in the business. They believe that IS is a career or specialisation in its own right, and for many who want to remain solely specialists throughout their career this may be true. However, if any such individual has ambitions to move even to the first-line management level (certainly to senior IS management levels) then they must understand the business and will not progress unless they do so.

So, is the fault at IS's door? It certainly sounds like it, but maybe it isn't – maybe the problem is that of the business's making and resolution.

4.1.2   Does the alignment problem belong to the business?

IS works throughout the business – it is unique because almost every part of the business is dependent upon its expertise and capabilities. You cannot say the same for Human Resource because it is the line managers that make people work and develop and control them. Human Resource is not called upon in the day-to-day use of human resource – to make people work, to keep people going, to develop and control them – but IS is responsible for IS resource.

Indeed if IS were like Human Resource and was thought of as 'IS Resource', IS management would be much simpler – just providing the resource and making line management make IS work. From the business viewpoint, that simply would not be appealing. The business knows it needs IS specialists and that line management need to call upon them as a matter of routine.

IS is unique. It operates throughout the corporate body and needs to be co-ordinated across the business for the business to be a whole. This needs co-ordinated business management to achieve this goal, which is the main problem. Most businesses do not have joined-up management in the manner that they need to give IS the direction it needs for IS to actively, quickly, flexibly, effectively and efficiently support the totality of the business.

IS needs the mechanics of business management to work more effectively in aligning the business with its IS. The business needs a management framework through which it manages all its functions and aligns the objectives and deliverables of the business functions to provide a unified outcome which IS can enable and support.

The business needs a management framework that aligns IS with the rest of the business, indeed aligns all parts of the business where alignment is needed.

> **Tip**
>
> **IS needs business management – more so than any other function – to operate effectively in order to do what the business wants of it.**

4.2 The mechanics of business management

In most organisations, business management is based on matrix management. When we say matrix management, people tend to think of project management. Project management is a form of matrix management that aligns people from different functional areas of the business and gets them to work together to achieve shared outcomes and to overcome functional boundaries. Project management involves a number of processes that enable the business to develop and implement change across functional boundaries.

The functional areas that projects bring together include the primary functions of the business, the elements of the Porter's value chain, i.e. inbound logistics, production, outbound logistics, sales and service. Projects also bring together the support functions of the business, i.e. business infrastructure, technology and human resource, that are used to develop and deliver the primary functions.

Chapter 3 consolidated the primary and secondary functional areas into the business value chains. Projects bring together the value chains so that the market need for products and services drives the development of the organisation's people, process and technology capabilities. Project management is vital to IS not just to manage the technology elements but also to align the IS development with the associated business developments of products, services, organisational capabilities, technology capabilities and the inevitable business process.

Without matrix management projects could not work for the business and IS would be unable to align with the business regarding business development and implementation initiatives.

Other examples of matrix management in the business are:

■ Business Planning, Budgeting and Financial Control operate across the business as a form of matrix management. People from different functions need to get together to agree plans, costs and resources where they affect each other or where they have a shared goal

■ Marketing, Sales, Production, Warehousing and Finance all need to get together to plan their part of a shared business plan.

Matrix management is an essential capability in business to pull the business together at different points in the business life cycle.

The business life cycle is the framework of management governance that pulls together the functions and value chains from 'Strategy to Delivery'.

All businesses have some form of management framework, whether formal or informal, rigorous or vague. However, there appears to be no standard management governance framework. It is surprising that − with all the governance problems experienced over the last few years, along with all the management books that have been written − there is little in the public domain on formal management governance frameworks. Certainly there are none that have related it to the alignment of the value chain or to the management of IS; those available focus only on elements of the mechanics of management such as projects and budgeting.

4.3 The management governance framework

The management governance framework is:

> **'The management framework and its processes by which a business directs, develops and delivers the products and services of the business.'**

It is the way that the Strategy is executed through business development products to develop product and service capabilities and through which day-to-day products and services are delivered and supported. It is the mechanism by which all the parts of the business and its supply chain partners work together on Strategy, Development and Operation.

Figure 4.1 illustrates the framework and what is involved in it. The framework is used to direct and run the business from left to right with feedback from right to left.

Typically the Strategy involves a long-term strategy; the Business Plan involves a short number of years with financial targets and budgets; the Business Architecture is the high-level design of the business, and so on.

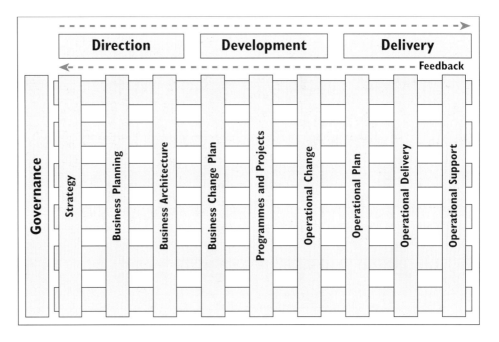

Figure 4.1 – The management governance framework

The business needs to provide unified Direction through disciplines and processes that involve Strategy, Business Plans, Budgets and Business Architecture.

The business needs to provide unified Development through a shared Business Change Plan and Development Programmes and Projects disciplines under the control of Operational Change disciplines in the Operational world.

The business needs to provide unified Delivery of products and services through shared Operational Planning, Operational Delivery and Operational Support.

The way the disciplines above are performed varies from business to business. Some businesses perform aspects formally and other aspects in an informal, ad-hoc manner. In terms of best practice business governance, the need for the individual disciplines above is crucial as is the way they interrelate. The governance framework formalises the touch points between the value chains. From both business and IS viewpoints, the best practice governance framework enables the processes and the relationships of the value chains to be formalised with each other across the governance model.

4.3.1 Unified matrix management framework – the governance view

Figure 4.2 illustrates the unified management matrix framework from the governance view where the business is managed from left to right through the governance framework, where Development and Delivery processes are driven from senior management's Direction processes.

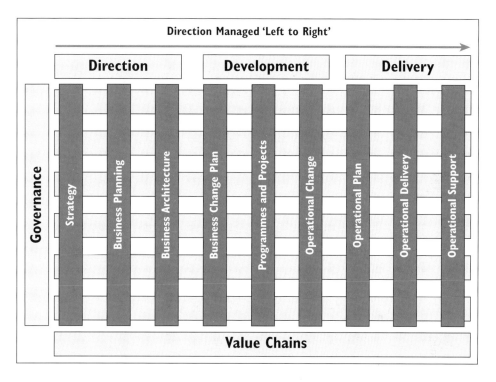

Figure 4.2 – The unified matrix management framework – the governance view

4.3.2 Unified matrix management framework – the value chain view

Similarly, Figure 4.3 illustrates the unified matrix management framework from top to bottom through the value chain framework – the market and customers drive the products and services that are needed, and this drives the needs of the business's capabilities, i.e. its People, Process and Technology, and the capabilities of its suppliers.

4.3.3 Business/IS alignment and the IS value chain view

Using Figure 4.4, matrix management can be applied to the alignment of IS with the business, such that IS is driven by the same management framework as the business. IS shares Direction, Development and Delivery disciplines and processes with the business.

For example, considering Development, IS development of its own people, process and technology is undertaken to support the business's people, processes and technology which are developed to support the business's products and services to support its market and customer development plans.

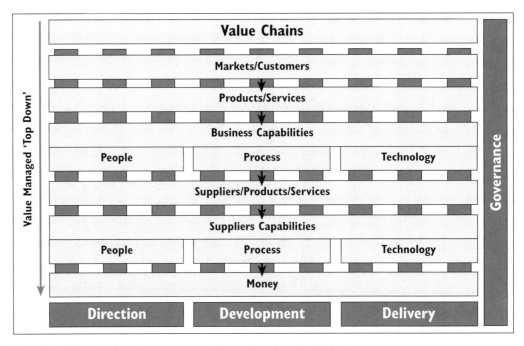

Figure 4.3 – The unified matrix management framework – the value chain view

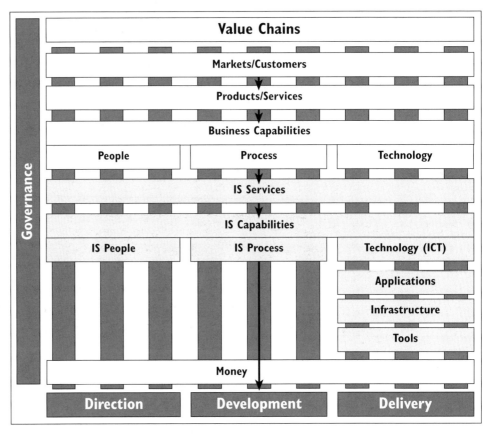

Figure 4.4 – The unified matrix management framework – the IS value chain view

IS is aligned with the business through the value chain relationships. IS services and capabilities support business services and business capabilities, notably business processes.

4.3.4   Business/IS touch points

So let's examine the IS touch points with the business around the Strategy, Planning and Architecture Governance processes as shown in Figure 4.5. In this we are looking at IS supporting Business Strategy development with IS being responsible for the strategy for IS service development to deliver and improve service delivery/operation and support capabilities.

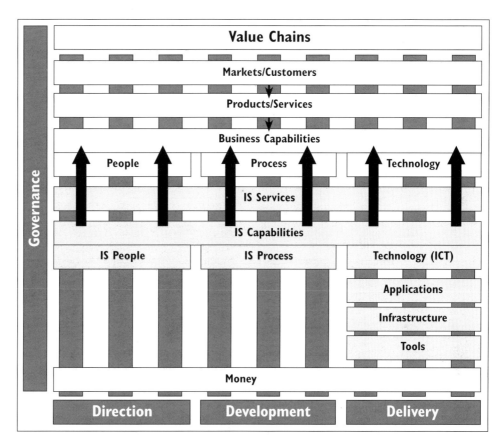

Figure 4.5 – Business/IS touch points

The business parties involved in business strategy are market, customer and product development strategists. These business people lead strategic thinking and are supported by business logistics strategists who are determining the strategies for in-house and third party business people, process and technology capabilities. When it comes to the development of business people, process and technology strategies, IS strategists need to work with their business strategy counterparts. This typically means that IS strategists have touch points with a combination of retail strategists, office strategists, distribution and warehousing strategists, manufacturing strategists, materials strategists and sourcing strategists as appropriate to the logistics and technologies deployed in an organisation and its suppliers/partners.

Each of the business strategists is responsible for the People, Process and Technology which need to be developed and deployed in their area of responsibility. The governance framework defines how these people work together and how Strategy turns into Business Architectures and then into Development Programmes and Operational Plans.

The process of developing IS strategies not only develops the ICT technologies but also the processes, organisation and sourcing/service provision options for IS. They undertake this under a common Strategy Governance process which is used by IS and by their business counterparts.

Example

If the business strategy involves developing the strategy for warehousing, then the IS strategist touch points are the warehousing strategists. They are looking for IS support to enable the warehousing technologies and processes to be fully effective through the provision of IS information and processing services, many of which will become embedded in the resulting warehousing operational capabilities.

The above is just an example of the IS touch points with the business, but it illustrates the reality that IS needs to engage with the business across the business governance framework, from IS Service Strategy development to IS Service Operation in support of Business Strategy to Business Operation.

4.3.5   The IS steering group

To ensure that business and IS strategies and plans remain synchronised, organisations need to form a joint co-ordinating body commonly called the IS Steering Group (ISG). This body consists of senior management representatives from various business areas and IS. The function of the ISG is to meet regularly and review both the business and IS plans and strategies to ensure that they are aligned as closely as possible to one another. In particular, the ISG is responsible for the activities outlined in Sections 4.7.1 to 4.7.3, and providing direction for all SIP activities.

The ISG normally has a remit that includes discussions on all aspects of the business involving IS service as well as proposed or possible change at a strategic level. Subjects for the ISG to discuss may include:

- **demand planning**: to identify any changes in demand for both short- and long-term planning horizons; such changes may be for both increases and decreases in demand, and concern both business-as-usual and projects

- **project authorisation and prioritisation**: to ensure that projects are authorised and prioritised to the mutual satisfaction of both the business and IS

- **review of projects**: to ensure that the expected benefits are being realised in accordance with project business cases and to identify whether the projects are on schedule

- **potential outsourcing**: to identify the need to outsource aspects of the IS service provision

- **business/IS strategy review**: to discuss major changes to business strategy and major proposed changes to ICT infrastructure

- **Business and IT Service Continuity**: the ISG, or a working party from the ISG, is responsible for aligning Business Continuity and IT Service Continuity strategies

- **policies and standards**: the ISG is responsible for ensuring that IS policies and standards, particularly in relation to financial strategy and performance management, are in place and aligned with the overall corporate vision and objectives.

4.4 Achieving alignment

It is essential to have clearly defined communication channels (or touch points) between IS and the business if business/IS alignment is to be achieved, as briefly discussed in Section 4.3.4. These channels need to be embedded within the IS operational processes so that regular communications take place to enable IS service providers to understand the drivers of the business and to enable the customers of IS to understand the potential of technology. As discussed later in this chapter, communication needs to take place at all levels within the organisation.

Despite the effort expended in strategic planning and business planning, it is often difficult to foresee or predict the future in terms of changes to business direction, priorities and new business needs and requirements. Such changes not only impact the business directly but also may have significant implications for existing relationships with service providers and partners.

Over the past few years there have been many high-profile examples where the business's IS needs have not been communicated to the service providers, resulting in the inability of IS to provide the required resources to meet those needs. It is also not unusual to find IS departments putting a work programme in place without any consideration to the priorities of the business, e.g. to refresh hardware and software. Sometimes it is purely coincidental if the programme of work happens to benefit the business as a whole and happens to meet the current needs of the customers. To resolve these issues and be sure that the needs of the business are being taken into consideration, then the following questions should be asked every time the IS service provider plans to make a change:

- How will this benefit the business?
- Is there something else that has a higher priority to the business?

Questions such as these should also be asked when considering any changes to the Service Management processes, reporting structure, organisation, technology or infrastructure.

An effective Business Perspective culture within IS ensures that business requirements are rapidly and accurately documented and communicated, and that IS services are aligned to those business requirements with the supplier elements underpinning and supporting that alignment. The Business Perspective approach has to deal with many different issues and conflicts that include:

- aligning IS with corporate objectives and strategies
- ensuring that personal objectives (and Personal Development Plans) for IS staff include alignment with the business
- ensuring that IS and business are using a common language/vocabulary
- developing relationships with both the business and suppliers
- balancing and compromising the often conflicting priorities and demands of different Business Units (each Business Unit thinks that its needs are greater than any other Business Unit)
- understanding, balancing, and reconciling individual Business Unit demands with corporate demands and objectives
- matching the service provider and supplier capabilities to the needs of the business and Business Units.

The business must work closely with the IS service providers to ensure that they respond in a timely and effective manner and react to changing business requirements. To sustain or improve the quality of service supplied, and cope with changing business requirements, close co-operation is required not only at operational and tactical levels, but also at the strategic level. It is necessary for the service providers to have visibility of the business strategy and plans so that they may align the IS strategy.

In the *Application Management* book there is further discussion of aligning the business and IS, including the Henderson and Venkatraman strategic business–IT alignment model, which provides a structured mechanism for beginning the thought processes of marrying the business and IS strategies.

The business/IS alignment as discussed above should be considered in relation to a conscious, structured mechanism of alignment or 'steering' towards business-focused goals, as discussed in Section 4.3. It must also take into account the organisation and culture (i.e. the ethos or attitude of the people) of the business and IS.

4.4.1   The business organisation and culture

Organisation

In every company, the business organisation is such that it supports the nature of the business being undertaken. However, in any customer/supplier relationship it is important for the customer to get the best possible service from the supplier. This applies equally to internal and external suppliers. One of the ways in which a customer can achieve this is by understanding the supplier's organisational structure and making appropriate adjustments to their own organisation to ensure that the appropriate communication channels are in place. This enables any potential (or actual) difficulties to be readily addressed and ensures that the customer's requirements are clearly articulated and understood.

Culture

Senior management describe the future of the business in terms of a business vision and this needs to be communicated, so that support can be readily gained from the various stakeholders. The achievement of business goals needs to be described with sufficient contextual information about how the vision might be implemented. This ensures that each element of the organisation has a culture that is compatible with the overall vision and is driven by the business imperatives and goals.

4.4.2   The IS organisation and culture

Organisation

One of the ways in which an IS organisation can ensure its effective service delivery to the business is by understanding the business's organisational structure and making appropriate adjustments to their own organisation to ensure that the appropriate communication channels are in place. An example of this is to ensure that the Business Relationship Managers (BRMs) and Service Delivery Managers are aligned to Business Units or lines of business. This enables any potential (or actual) difficulties to be readily addressed and ensures that the business's requirements are clearly articulated and understood.

It is very easy for the IS organisation to be concerned with technology without putting the appropriate emphasis on the culture and people skills of the staff. It is vitally important that all members of the IS organisation have a good appreciation of the business structure, products and drivers. One way this can be achieved is by ensuring that members of the IS organisation attend business induction courses. The IS organisation needs to ensure staff have the appropriate service skills as well as the technical skills they may require. As an example most organisations train their Service Desk staff to use the technology they have on the desk, and to support the technology the customers have. However, these same organisations often assume their Service Desk staff naturally have the appropriate interpersonal and telephone skills, and don't give them training to improve their ability to do this very important aspect of their job. As stated previously, having good communications channels enables alignment of IS and the business so it is important that this is borne in mind when the IS organisational structure is put in place.

Culture

The culture of the IS organisation needs to be such that all IS staff understand the nature of the business and recognise their contribution to the business goals and strategy. To achieve this, it is necessary that the IS goals and strategy are developed in conjunction with, and aligned to, the business goals and strategy. Obviously, there may be a variety of different cultures within the business organisation, for example where there are a number of distinct companies that comprise the whole organisation. In these circumstances, it is necessary for the IS organisation to be sufficiently flexible to be able to align with many different business cultures.

4.5 Establishing the IS direction

To establish the IS direction needed to achieve the goals of the business-aligned IS strategy, it is necessary to:

- set strategic objectives
- assess the current position
- perform a gap analysis
- ensure continued alignment.

4.5.1 Set the strategic objectives

IS must develop a robust vision (setting the future IS direction aligned with that of the business). Once this has been established the strategic objectives can be set. The purpose of these is to provide a framework against which the current IS services can be assessed and any gaps identified and prioritised. It is essential to communicate the vision and objectives throughout IS.

4.5.2 Assess current position

To assess the current position, there are a number of techniques that are available. However, the most useful fall into one of two categories: benchmarking, and maturity modelling. More details of the specific techniques can be found in the *Planning to Implement Service Management* book, Chapter 3.

The customer is also able to gauge the current level of support and IS service provided to the business. This can be achieved through monitoring service levels using Service Management reporting mechanisms and the results of customer satisfaction surveys. All of these are important parameters for measuring the effectiveness of the Business Perspective approach in IS. However, other factors need to be considered; these include the IS response to environmental changes that might necessitate a change in business direction.

It is likely that an organisation may need to use a combination of techniques to establish a clear view of the current position. Whichever technique (or selection of techniques) is used, it is important to establish a clear scope and terms of reference for the exercise. The aim of the assessment is to ensure that the IS organisation is following industry best practice and to concentrate on identifying the degree to which a Business Perspective approach is in place. It is also essential to ensure that the assessment evaluates how well the IS organisation is aligned to business-focused goals.

Tip

In circumstances where the business perception of IS is extremely poor, then neither benchmarking nor maturity modelling should be carried out. Where the business feels that IS is not delivering quality services, or is poor value for money, any attempt to carry out benchmarking or maturity modelling will be seen as a pointless exercise (or even a defensive reaction). In these cases, it is better to engage with the customers and identify their perception of IS.

Benchmarking

Viewed from a Business Perspective, benchmark measurements can help the organisation to assess IS services, performance and spend against peer or competitor organisations and best practice, both across the whole of IS and by appropriate business areas, answering questions such as:

- How does IS spend compare to other similar organisations – overall, as a percentage of revenue, or per employee?
- How does IS spend compare for similar functions, e.g. payroll functions either within an organisation or with other organisations?
- How does IS spend compare across Business Units or business processes?
- How does IS spend compare across locations or technologies?
- How effective is IS service delivery (and identify opportunities and measures for improvement)?
- Which is the most appropriate sourcing option?
- Is the value of a long-term sourcing contract being maintained year on year?

Benchmarking activities need to be business-aligned. They can be expensive exercises whether undertaken internally or externally, and therefore they need to be focused on where they can deliver most value.

For internal service providers, cost benchmarking can assess the efficiency and effectiveness of the IS unit. For external service providers, especially outsourced services, they can help to ensure the right IS services for the right price. Results of benchmarking not only provide a statement of performance, but can also be used to identify, recommend and plan improvements. They can also demonstrate value to the business and set targets for improvement levels, with subsequent benchmarking to assess achievement.

Comparisons of service performance and workload characteristics between peer organisations, the effectiveness of business process, and the IS contribution to IS are also of value as part of a Total Cost of Ownership (TCO) assessment. Third party specialists are available to conduct benchmarking and assessments, giving the business an external perspective and helping to lend credibility to the results and recommendations for improvements.

There is a variety of IS benchmarking available separately or in combination, including:

- cost and performance for internal service providers
- price and performance for external service providers
- process performance against industry best practice
- financial performance of high-level IS costs against industry or peers
- effectiveness considering satisfaction ratings and business alignment at all levels.

The context for benchmarking requires information about the organisation's profile, complexity and relative comparators. An effective and meaningful profile contains four key components:

- **company information profile**: the company profile defines the landscape of an organisation, i.e. basic information on the company size, industry type, geographic location and types of user are typical of data gathered to establish this profile
- **current assets**: the IS assets mix within the organisation may include production IS, desktop and mobile clients, peripherals, network and server assets
- **current best practices**: these include policies, procedures and/or tools that improve returns, and their maturity and degree of usage
- **complexity**: complexity includes information about the end-user community, the types and quantities of varied technologies in use and how IS is managed.

The main advantages of benchmarking are:

- it may take less time to complete than a maturity modelling exercise
- it may help to identify 'quick wins' which can be incorporated into a Service Improvement Programme (SIP)
- it can help improve the business confidence in IS by showing a willingness to identify and adopt marketplace best practice.

However, each organisation's culture is likely to be different. This means that benchmarking may not identify some key areas where the Business Perspective approach is falling short.

Maturity modelling

This allows the organisation to compare its current state against a set of criteria (normally using some form of questionnaire). There are many different types of maturity model, but each has a largely similar set of criteria and levels of maturity (see *Planning to Implement Service Management* book for further details).

The maturity model approach is an excellent means of communicating to the non-IS community IS's readiness (or not) to deliver the desired level of service. It provides a non-technical framework which can then be used to show exactly how the components of an IS organisation's portfolio relate to specific degrees of maturity/readiness. It can also help to highlight that in most instances one cannot jump straight to a fully operational Business Perspective model in a single leap. It generally needs an evolutionary approach.

The main advantages of maturity modelling are:

- it has a highly structured framework and methodology
- it may provide a clearer view of the steps needed to achieve improvement since the maturity models are based on a series of well-defined levels.

Maturity modelling may require more time and effort than benchmarking.

4.5.3 Perform a gap analysis

Once the current position has been assessed, the gaps between the current position and the IS vision and strategic objectives are identified. The impact of these gaps on the IS and business strategy needs assessment to be able to prioritise any initiatives/improvements that may be required.

4.5.4 Ensure continued alignment

Prioritised initiatives to close any gaps need to be undertaken to bring a closer alignment between IS and the business. However, part of the ongoing responsibility of IS is to monitor the service quality to ensure that alignment continues.

A technique which is frequently used to monitor and measure the services being provided to the business by IS is the Balanced Scorecard (BSC). Further information on the BSC is available at www.balancedscorecard.com and in the Balanced Scorecard Functional Standards, Balanced Scorecard Collaborative, Inc. at www.bscol.com, from which a sample BSC has been included in Appendix B.1. The BSC is used to identify the multiple aspects of the services which must be realised. By picking the appropriate business-aligned measures to be used in the BSC, IS can identify activities that need to be included in a continuous service improvement plan to ensure alignment is maintained/improved.

Crucial to the whole idea of the Business Perspective approach is the need to cover all aspects and elements of the IS services. This is totally sympathetic to the BSC approach of seeking, understanding and taking account of all the influences and beneficiaries of a service. There is widespread adoption of the specific and defined concepts of the BSC but, for the Business Perspective approach, understanding it rests upon the realisation that the IS internal processes represent, in BSC terms, only one of four independent perspectives of influence and involvement for IS services.

IS can use this technique to set objectives within all four perspectives of the BSC:

- customer: meeting the needs of customers in highly competitive markets
- financial: meeting the objectives of the stakeholders
- internal processes: achieving on the key levers that drive performance excellence
- learning and growth: meeting the expectations and building up the capabilities of employees whose skills determine the organisation's future.

It is crucial that any objectives within these four areas are aligned to those within the appropriate Business Units and the overall corporate objectives. Critical Success Factors (CSFs) and Key Performance Indicators (KPIs) need to be established to measure the success in meeting these

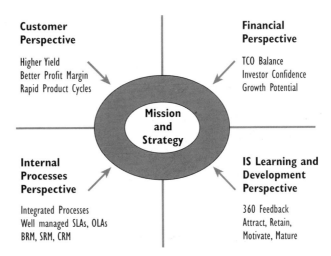

Figure 4.6 – A Balanced Scorecard concept

objectives. All of these measures are, wherever possible, business- or customer-defined measurements. This includes the use of customer satisfaction surveys and customer effectiveness surveys, as well as feedback and comments received from service reviews and other customer meetings.

4.6 Alignment levels: strategic, tactical and operational

A fundamental part of delivering service is to ensure that the services being delivered are aligned to and underpin the business needs of the customers. With the higher profile of IS and greater business dependency on IS services, there is a requirement to ensure that throughout the service provider's organisation all interaction with, and effort on behalf of, the customer is aligned to the customer needs.

The motivations for IT Service Management are well documented within the ITIL framework. It must also be understood that true business/IS alignment can only be achieved by:

- generating an increased understanding of the organisation's business and its needs
- establishing and developing a trusting relationship at a strategic level
- identifying and responding to business requirements at an early stage, e.g. corporate agility is often reliant on IS being able to respond rapidly to new and changing business needs in new and changing marketplaces
- improving the two-way communication flow between the business and IS
- providing a conduit for business-related information back into IS
- delivering business benefit by identifying opportunities for the increased exploitation of IS services
- defining measures/KPIs which are understood and are relevant to business management
- developing a greater understanding of how the ICT infrastructure has penetrated into business processes.

There is therefore a need to establish, develop and maintain close trusted professional relationships with the business at all levels. This can be achieved through the implementation of effective relationship management as part of the Business Perspective approach.

Effective business/IS alignment can only be achieved if all parts of both business and service provider organisations are included and considered. This leads us to look more closely at the structural levels within organisations.

4.6.1 Alignment activities

Organisations can be said to operate at three key levels: strategic, tactical and operational, and there are specific corporate functions at each level. For IS to be fully aligned with the business, interactions must also take place at the same three levels.

There are a number of activities that need to be performed at all three levels to achieve business/IS alignment. Necessarily, these tend to focus more at the strategic level but activities at all three levels are required.

Table 4.1 shows, for each of the three levels, the high-level corporate functions and the corresponding activities that need to take place to ensure that service providers align themselves and their services to the organisation's needs.

Table 4.1 – Key alignment activities at each level

Level	Corporate function	Alignment activities
Strategic	Setting policy and direction	Understand the high level relationship between the business and IS
		Understand the business policy and direction
		Educate senior staff on the benefits and application of new technologies
		Interpret high-level business needs and translate them into IS requirements
		Implement ICT systems and services which underpin the organisation's business needs
		Communicate pertinent information to all within the service provider's organisation
		Align business, IS and major supplier vision, strategies, plans, goals and objectives
		Analyse and identify value chains, critical processes and Vital Business Functions (VBFs are described under Availability Management in the *Service Delivery* book)
Tactical	Planning and implementing business change	Ensure change programmes are fully integrated and aligned with the business strategy through close working with the business/IS interface in Change Management, Project Management, Service Level Management, Capacity Management and Financial Management
		Undertake medium-term planning and alignment of business, IS and major supplier tactical plans, goals and objectives
		Undertake project and change scheduling based on business need, impact and urgency

Level	Corporate function	Alignment activities
Tactical	Planning and implementing business change	Enable medium-term cost and risk reduction
		Deliver technical migration projects (e.g. network upgrade or desktop replacement)
		Deliver incremental change
Operational	Delivering day-to-day operational business needs	Ensure that all service provider staff are aware of and work towards achieving and maintaining the delivery of the aligned systems and services
		Understand the context of the IS operational function within the wider business function and its alignment to business priority
		Undertake supply chain analysis and establish the role of IS groups and suppliers
		Establish ITIL processes and their alignment to their equivalents within the business (i.e. Change Management aligned with Business Change Management, IT Service Continuity Management aligned with Business Continuity Management, Financial Management of IT aligned with Business Financial Planning)
		Improve service delivery by understanding, positioning and adapting the IS service(s) according to its context within the business
		Reduce operational costs and risks by close association of Business Continuity Management and IT Service Continuity Management or Financial Management of IT with Business Financial Planning

It is important to note that, at all levels, effective communication and interaction between the IS and its customers is paramount.

The way many organisations achieve good customer interaction is to adopt techniques such as Carlsson's 'Moment of Truth' philosophy. These techniques involve identifying each customer interaction with the IS service provider and then implementing all cost-justifiable activities to make each encounter as simple, easy, enjoyable and as efficient as possible. This can be achieved by:

- keeping close to customers and talking to them on a regular basis
- encouraging all front-line staff involved in customer contact and interactions to provide feedback information on problem areas or areas of weakness, including suggestions for improvement
- regularly experiencing the customer journey and/or the customer experience
- reviewing processes from the customer experience and the business's perspective on a regular basis.

The main activities at the strategic and tactical levels are discussed in a little more detail below.

Influence business and IS decision-making

For effective business/IS alignment there is a need for access to information relating to the business, its mission, goals and objectives. Effective relationship management can collect this valuable information and make it available to IS.

For effective business/IS alignment there is a need to influence both sides to ensure the most appropriate route is taken to meet the overall organisation objectives. This is particularly true at the strategic level. A major task within this activity is the establishment of relationship and communications plans. In addition, IS needs to be actively involved in marketing its services and capabilities to the business.

Understand the business strategy

Those working towards business/IS alignment must be fully aware of the overall business strategy and the plans of business areas, which include the IS strategic plans.

Example

It is possible that the business wishes to expand its available channels by exploiting e-commerce. The role of IS is to assist in identifying how this strategy can be achieved. The IS strategy needs to include the appropriate elements that support the future business direction. This includes appropriate hardware as well as any additional capacity needed to support the expected business demand.

The business strategy may be to minimise investment in all forms of technology (including IS). However, IS may wish to continue updating the infrastructure to relatively new technology to minimise support costs. Effective business/IS alignment enables reconciliation of these conflicting strategies to achieve the best option for the entire organisation.

The ISG must play an important role in the alignment of business and IS strategies as depicted in Figure 4.7.

Understand the business policy

The high-level policies that underpin the organisation's strategy must be clearly understood so that Business Units and IS can be influenced and guided to work within such policies.

IS Portfolio Management

At the strategic level a portfolio can be defined as a suite of IS-enabled business change programmes managed to optimise overall enterprise value. Portfolio Management is an integrated set of processes, techniques and tools that, when consistently applied to the portfolio of programmes, allows for:

- selection of investments targeted at those areas that yield the greatest return
- effective programme planning and execution of those programmes to return the greatest possible value to the business
- ongoing governance and active management of the portfolio ensuring the business benefits promised by the investments are realised.

Portfolio Management can and should also be applied to the overall management of IS service provision as covered in Section 5.3, and at the application level, as detailed in the *Application Management* book.

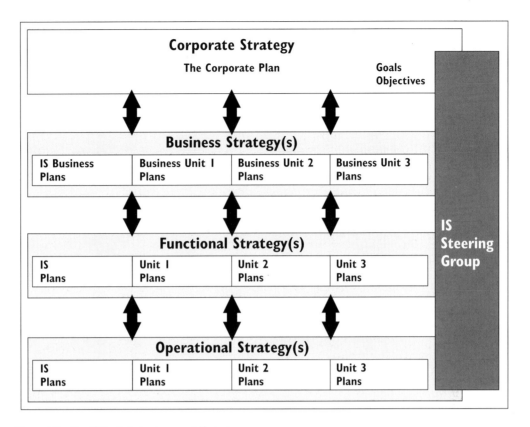

Figure 4.7 – The ISG role in business and IS strategy

Resource deployment

The tactical deployment of IS staff resources is another contributing factor to the success of good customer/IS relationships. Staff resource is finite, so resources must be used in a manner that is aligned to business priority and maximises the benefit to the organisation.

Establish true support for business processes

At an operational level the development of best practice IS processes is completed in conjunction with clearly identified objectives that ensure the services being delivered are truly aligned with and support the business needs. Each person in IS should be able to identify which business processes they are supporting. This means that there is a need to develop an overall culture that is business-aligned and business-focused at all levels of the IS organisation.

Establish sound supplier relationship management

IS must manage the relationship with suppliers and ensure that the needs of the business (as identified in its plans and strategy) are taken into account when establishing and underpinning contracts. It also ensures that suppliers gain a greater awareness of the organisation's business.

Service continuity and business alignment

It is not uncommon to find IS managers putting IS continuity measures in place in isolation and equally it is not uncommon to find Business Continuity Plans that do not consider the dependency on IS. There is little benefit in developing one without the other so when putting plans in place it is essential for business managers and IS managers to work together to ensure that fully integrated and tested Business Continuity Plans are developed that incorporate IS service provisions. IT Service Continuity Management is in fact a sub-set of Business Continuity Management.

All changes to the business and to the ICT infrastructure, including processes, must be assessed for their impact on current Business and IT Service Continuity provisions. This must be done as early in the planning cycle as possible for there to be time to implement and test any changes.

The process of IT Service Continuity and integration into Business Continuity is discussed in detail in the *Service Delivery* book. The process includes developing a strategy after conducting a Business Impact Analysis (see an example in Appendix B.5) to ascertain the impact of loss of service on the business and a risk analysis to identify threats to components of the infrastructure and the vulnerability of the organisation if these threats are realised. The strategy normally includes risk reduction measures as well as strategic recovery options and is based on the overall needs of the business, not the capability of IS.

Best practice guidance on BCM is available in the *PAS 56 Guide to Business Continuity Management* from the British Standards Institution (BSi) and the Business Continuity Institute (BCI).

4.7 Financial Management

The Business Perspective approach requires IS (whether it is a cost centre or a profit centre) effectively to behave as a unit of the overall business. It must also operate within the same governance framework as the business, and be run on business-like lines. That means that it must be run on sound financial lines (as any other Business Unit). In this section, we examine three elements of Financial Management:

- Total Cost of Ownership
- Return on Investment
- Planning.

Financial Management is discussed in more detail in the *Service Delivery* book.

4.7.1 Total Cost of Ownership

Total Cost of Ownership (TCO) principles and methods can place the business value chain into perspective. To measure TCO effectively, the first place to begin is with best practices of Financial Management for IS services. You must first know what IS services cost, how they relate to each area of the business and the translation of those costs into IS services measured in business metrics.

TCO is one tool in a suite of tools that together form the business/IS value measurements. Like any best practice, TCO has a cyclical, repeatable flow as illustrated in Figure 4.8.

TCO measures the direct and indirect costs of the IS environment and then equates them against the expected business outcomes to produce a Return on Investment (ROI) indicator.

Most IS TCO models have the same basic high-level elements of measurement categories:

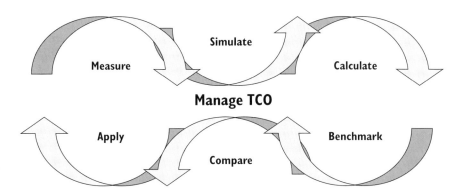

Figure 4.8 – The TCO cycle

■ direct costs – those identified in traditional IS budgets

– hardware and software
– operations
– administration

■ indirect costs – those costs generated from IS users

– downtime
– depreciation cost metrics
– end-user operations.

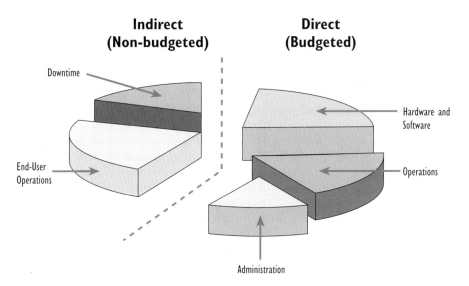

Figure 4.9 – Distributed computing TCO model (adapted from Gartner's model)

Carrying out a TCO exercise typically demonstrates that the true costs of IS, specifically at the desktop, are on average five times more than the costs of acquisition. Most of this cost is attributed not to technology, but to ongoing Service Management processes.

As discussed earlier in this chapter, assessment of TCO may be included in a benchmarking exercise since many organisations wish to view their cost profile against that of other comparable organisations. The numbers do not have value until they are seen in context, i.e. considered against other TCO benchmarked organisations, or against previous measurements for the same organisation to establish progress (or regression).

Tip

A common myth in the IT industry is that the objective is to achieve a lower TCO. This perspective can serve to undermine the value of IS by encouraging unrealistic constraints on IS resources for the sake of a low TCO. The true objective is to have the 'right' TCO for your business and IS value. Simply lowering TCO may have adverse affects on business value activities. Much like the concept of demand management for capacity management planning, the right TCO that is cost-effective without sacrificing value is the best objective.

4.7.2 Return on Investment

The majority of IS budgets are spent on installed applications, but it seems that most of the discussion is around new spending. It's understandable, but viewing infrastructure and applications as a Portfolio of Services (see Section 5.3) can expose important trends and lead to dramatically different conclusions.

Linking your IS services and assets with the business organisation through the services provided to users helps expose these trends. Services can be grouped by profit centres that align with those used in the business to illustrate the IS value to the business in a way that has tangible meaning to the business. To achieve this, the Business Relationship Manager works directly with customers to group their inventory of services into logical 'suites of service' so they can be understood by both IS and the business in a meaningful way. This gives customers an understanding of which services are delivering the greatest value.

Measuring service suites using the cost of ownership benchmark cycle (see Figure 4.8) then shows the ROI by service and identifies opportunities for improvement from a cost, customer satisfaction and IS management perspective.

4.7.3 Planning

IS must synchronise its planning cycle with that of the business in the same way as other Business Units. For all Business Units it is likely (if not certain) that there is an annual planning cycle that is iterative between:

- the annual planning process
- understanding the business demand plan for the Business Unit's resources
- defining the supply plan for the Business Unit's resources.

For IS, the annual planning process normally delivers two major outputs:

- **Strategic Plan**: typically covers a period of up to five years and describes the strategic direction IS will follow to support its customers and their business strategy. It sets the direction to ensure that IS meets the requirements of its customers and is positioned for future developments. The IS Strategic Plan is a subset of the Business Strategic Plan.

- **Annual Operational Plan**: describes the workload of IS within the coming year based on agreed levels of:
  - contracted services

    –   project activity with approved business sponsorship

    –   demand for standard service requests (i.e. requests for services which are defined in the IS Service Catalogue with predefined costs, implementation/installation procedures and which have been authorised as standard services by the IS Change Manager).

The outputs are developed through discussion with the IS customers in management forums (such as the ISG), and formalised Business Relationship Management meetings. The strategic and operational plans reflect the needs of customers, as well as internal operational requirements (e.g. service continuity testing).

IS need to confirm the following with its customers:

- current levels of agreed services and any proposed amendments
- strategic business initiatives that IS need to support in the future
- current business change plans which need to be supported
- internal initiatives required to support the strategic direction (e.g. customer-sponsored initiatives to improve service and reduce costs).

Business cases for internal initiatives are presented to the business to get approval for the initiatives to be carried out as projects.

The IS Strategic Plan is one of the key inputs into the development of the Operational Plan, and both are used as key communication tools between IS and its customers. The Operational Plan reflects both the operational and financial aspects of IS activities for the forthcoming business year. This plan forms the basis for the different IS department plans, the demand plan, the supply plan, and the annual operating budget.

5 UNDERSTANDING THE BUSINESS VIEWPOINT

The purpose of this chapter is to aid the manager working within the IS service provider organisation to understand the perceptions and attitudes that are held by their customers and users working within the Business Units supported by the delivered IS services. While other parts of this book deal with approaches, processes and procedures to harmonise IS and business goals, this chapter concentrates on the need for the IS service provider to understand how the business views the services they use and the context within which they use those services.

This means that the ideas within this chapter do not map elegantly into strategic, tactical and operational components, but are more cross-categorical in concept. In many instances, an understanding of the main principles of the business strategy informs and influences the tactical and operational elements of service provision.

Internal conflicts within Business Units, and between Business Unit and corporate objectives, are to be expected, and IS provision must steer a path between potentially conflicting demands.

Understanding the customer's perspective – to see, feel and care about things as they do – seems a simple and sensible objective to state, but on investigation, requires significant and extensive effort to achieve, and even more to maintain on a day-to-day basis. Specifically, achieving the understanding requires the traditional IS service provider to question many things, especially many attitudes, that they take for granted.

5.1　Why the business view is different

It is relatively common in many industries for staff to transfer from the business operations to the IS service provider and vice versa. Those staff remain employed by the same company and continue to contribute to the same overall objective. However, certainly in most organisations, the views and attitudes of those working directly in the business (being supported by service providers) differ significantly from those within IS (doing the supporting).

Working in different areas, contributing different elements to delivery of the goals, results in different perspectives. These different perspectives are important – the aim here is not to convert IS people into people better suited to carry out front-line tasks, and certainly not to suggest that an organisation would work better with homogeneity amongst their staff – some kind of uniformly average people, widely informed and versatile. Many organisations' survival relies on specialist and dedicated skills, in both the service provider and internal customer. Rather it is to suggest that a degree of understanding of the customer environment and business drivers among IS people will lead to the delivery of IS services which can be built, maintained and targeted more appropriately.

People have different jobs to do, and so adapt their ideas and behaviour to those tasks. Different tasks attract people with appropriate skills, which accentuate the differences in attitude between the two groups. Each group has their drivers and constraints, with deep knowledge of the environments within which they work. IS cannot expect customers to have total understanding of the IS service provider's business, nor is it reasonable to expect the IS service provider to understand fully all the nuances of the customer's daily business. But an understanding of the general requirements and, crucially, the reasons for doing things in a particular way can go a long way towards delivering requirements.

5.1.1 Business views on risk

One area that illustrates the difference in attitudes and the need for understanding of the business context is that of business risk. Traditionally IS seek assurances of success, or at least the absence of failure, before authorising a change to or release of a business service. Attention is centred on releases, of hardware, software documentation, etc., and being assured of delivering as specified.

The business is much more interested in potential (but less than guaranteed) benefit and advantage.

> **Example**
>
> In one volatile and competitive business environment, the UK mobile telephone supply business, customers asked IS if they were now able to implement a much needed change to the business software. IS replied that it could not go into the next change slot, because there was still a 30% risk of failure. Business reaction was to insist on implementation, for in their eyes a 70% chance of success, and the concomitant business advantage was, without any hesitation, the right and smart move. Very few of their business initiatives had that high a chance of success.
>
> The point is that the risk and gamble of the business environment (selling mobile telephones) had not been understood within IS, and inappropriate (i.e. IS) rules had been applied.
>
> The dominant risk is the business one and that should have been sought, established, understood and applied by the service provider. Sensibly, of course, this might well be accompanied by documentation of the risk-based decision – covering one's back perhaps – but nonetheless the need remains to understand the Business Perspective and act accordingly.

This example illustrates that all risk assessment must, finally, be tied back to the general business risk. Every element of the organisation relies on that organisation's survival for its own continued existence. Within a service provider, the risks focused on tend to be the risks to the continued successful delivery of that service. The risk to the business is of a fundamentally different nature: a possibility of improvement, to be balanced against the cost of disruption should the change fail. Indeed the business benefits themselves are based on a structure of assumptions and risks, of which the success or failure of IS is but one element. The IS view of risk is traditionally a simple 'What is the chance of it working?' This risk factor is likely to be balanced against possible benefits accruing from success.

Having been trained in binary arithmetic, logic and theories such as 'zero defects', the programmers view is very often that it either works properly, or if it doesn't it has to be fixed before it can go 'live'. In the past the IS department has been heavily criticised for systems that are late or slow or error-prone, and when long development cycles were more acceptable they exercised the power of veto on putting systems or changes 'live'. The Business Perspective ensures that there is a much more pragmatic view of risk in these situations than historically was the case.

It can, in practice, be hard to achieve and to demonstrate to others (e.g. management and finance roles) that a larger perspective for risk assessment is appropriate. The modern affectation for smaller cost centres and judging performance in terms of meeting local budget targets can deflect organisations from the correct assessment of business risk. In the public sector the scope for relevant risk can be very large indeed, with political considerations and the knock-on effect of changes to public services, benefit payments, etc.

As well as the normal business measure (monetary) one can see how other drivers such as legislative change, the possibility of hitting immovable deadlines, etc. would make 'risk-taking' the right move. This is also demonstrative of how an appreciation of the business strategy (a propensity for risk-taking) translates into appropriate tactical behaviour by IS.

5.1.2 The service provider in context

One of the common causes of ineffective service delivery is where service providers take an IS-centric view of the situation. Lack of a Business Perspective means that this is done unconsciously, with no realisation that there could be any other possible view of things. IS service providers often confuse the true situation 'The business processes require IS service' with the often false premise – 'IS is the reason business processes work'.

In practice, of course, the business processes rely on multiple supporting services, with IS being the crucial provider, or one of the key ones. But there are other key service providers and IS needs to be able to see their place in that bigger picture. In many situations, a considerable improvement in the overall quality of the business process can be achieved by collaboration, co-operation, and above all communication, between the multiple service providers upon which the business processes depend.

Understanding the situation from the Business Perspective involves seeing the roles that those multiple providers take, and working towards the overall efficiency and effectiveness of the integrated set of processes.

> **Tip**
>
> **Good service providers seek out and collaborate with fellow service providers to the same customer area. They can understand and make all balances and connections.**
>
> **One example of this is being tried within a Scandinavian hospital environment, where IS and medical technical staff are collaborating to provide the technological support to medical practitioners. Suggestions have been made for bringing the two groups under a single management structure to facilitate the collaboration.**

Collaboration between multiple suppliers to the business can make a significant contribution towards the quality of the end product, and the ease with which the service is delivered. It is neither practical nor efficient to rely on the customer, internal or external, to be aware of all the combinations and supplier interactions and interdependencies.

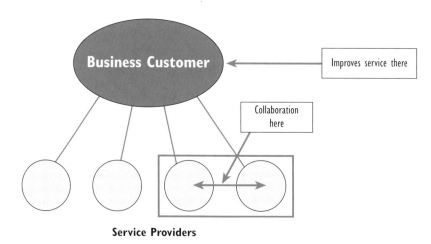

Figure 5.1 – A collaborative approach

Figure 5.1 is illustrative only and shows the idea only in the simplest schematic form. In practice a degree of collaboration usually exists, perhaps initiated by one or other of the service providers, or more likely required by the customer. The real benefits come from the right level of mutual understanding and awareness of each other's needs, constraints and attitudes. In some circumstances the choice of supplier may have been influenced by factors important to the customer, but not meaningful to other suppliers, e.g. political or contractual influences. In these circumstances the suppliers have no practical option other than to accept the situation and collaborate to deliver the best possible end-result for their shared customer.

5.2 Understanding relationships

Relationship management is concerned with ensuring that the right degree of communication and facilitation takes place to enable the delivery of the optimum level of service from the service provider to the customer. This communication includes:

- meetings to review performance and requirements
- reporting of performance against agreed criteria
- review of costs, charges and budgets
- customer and supplier surveys
- updates on changes in business circumstances, constraints, preferences, etc. and supplier relationships.

The mechanics of establishing and maintaining supplier relationships are dealt with in Chapter 7.

5.2.1 Supplier management and business management

Many of the essential elements of relationship management fall under the term of 'internal account management' in many organisations. Whether there is a designated separate account management role, or whether the processes are covered under the aegis of Service Management, Service Level Management, etc. is academic. What matters is that the necessary communication channels are created, maintained and used to deliver the understanding of the business that is necessary to deliver appropriate IS services. Merely establishing the idea will not deliver the benefits; ongoing effort and responsibility are required in adapting the procedures to changing circumstance.

It must be recognised that this effort costs resources, people and money, and the resources must be budgeted for. This commitment applies to both the supplier and the customer – indeed almost everyone performs both roles, playing their part in the supply and value chains – looking in both directions along those chains.

Relationship management addresses the two related aspects of Supplier Relationship Management and Business Relationship Management. The IS service provider role logically fits between suppliers, delivering goods or services to the service provider, and the customer who receives services. Both the suppliers and the customer may be internal or external to the service provider's organisation. External relationships are formalised via a contract, internal ones by a Service or Operational Level Agreement.

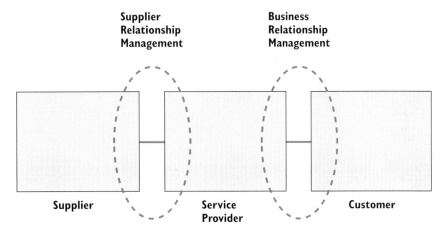

Figure 5.2 – A simplified representation of the relationships (source: BS 15000: 2003 Part 2)

The service provider fulfils a role within a supply chain, where each step in the chain adds benefit, with the service provider receiving services or goods from the supplier and delivering an enhanced service to the customer. The concepts of value chain and its applicability in understanding the Business Perspective are addressed in Chapter 3.

These relationships comprise multiple players, taking roles both as suppliers and customers and with business connections between many of them directly, as well as via the service provider. Good relationship processes between all parties ensure:

- business needs are understood and their delivery monitored
- all appropriate capabilities and constraints are identified, monitored and understood, especially those arriving from changing business needs and constraints
- responsibilities and obligations are appreciated and reported on.

Although staff may consider themselves as suppliers in their day-to-day jobs, we are, in everyday life, all customers. This awareness of how it feels to have needs and seek their fulfilment is an experience we all have, which enables us to see the Business Perspective. For a service provider to deliver appropriately to all customers, and other stakeholders, requires all those stakeholders to be identified, together with their expectations and how they perceive the services being delivered and supported. Only when relevant parties and their expectations have been identified can steps to deliver those expectations be meaningfully taken.

Both supplier behaviour and customer perception is influenced by the nature of the relationship, e.g. is it a monopoly, typically an internal provider that the customer has to use, or is there free choice, or at least the perception of free choice, such as an outsourced IS supplier?

Axioms such as 'the customer is king' are rightly regarded as outdated and simplistic, with the emphasis shifting towards partnerships delivering benefits to both parties. However, we should still recognise that, typically, the relationship exists to deliver, for supplier profit (not necessarily monetary), the requirements of the customer.

That is how most customers perceive the situation, and so the supplier must be aware of that perception and adapt their performance to support that perception.

5.2.2 Reaching agreements

Two parties (or more) are involved in negotiation and communication – the supplier(s) and the customer. The different requirements, constraints and expectations that each party has need to be reconciled into a common set of understandings that describe, predict and measure the service delivered.

Achieving this agreement requires each party to change their initial stance, and this 'coming together' requires communication, typically by negotiation between representatives.

Effective negotiation

For effective negotiation to take place it is necessary for each group to have:

- authorised representatives to speak for the group at meetings and other communications
- the requisite knowledge of their group's needs, absolute requirements, desires and available resources
- an appropriate degree of perception of the other party's situation (i.e. IS needs some business perception; customers need some awareness of supplier perception)
- the desire to reach agreement based upon common goals (e.g. the overall profit of the organisation to which both groups belong)
- the realisation that negotiation is not a competitive activity – in many supplier/customer relationships all parties are working for the same organisation and their future successes are bound together, in which case, excessive competitiveness can be damaging to the organisation's overall viability.

The theory of negotiation typically talks in terms of two parties capable of decision and execution between those two groups. The real-life situation is often far more complicated, with multiple players, not all represented together, and compromises reached between some groups that require adjustments to supporting agreements.

This all takes time, an understanding of the bigger picture and the organisational skills to consider all relevant aspects and apply them properly to the situation.

Whilst many deals seem to be agreed quickly and easily at meetings, often the apparent ease of final negotiation hides considerable preliminary work, done with smaller groups and key individuals beforehand. And it pays to be aware that suppliers of other services to your customer e.g. office services, production control, or personnel, will probably discuss matters that affect your negotiating position.

Much of the most effective discussion takes place informally, at a level not recognised by official communication channels, where the level of knowledge and understanding facilitates effective transfer of requirements and deliverables.

Example

In a UK government organisation there had been a long-running issue over the delivery of information to the Finance division by the IS department. Finance had formally requested reports in a particular format and at a specified frequency. IS had dismissed the requirement as impractical, and after several months the stalemate prevailed and both sides felt aggrieved.

The issue was finally resolved during an inter-section cricket match one Wednesday evening. Finance had a good bowler, and IS's batsmen were dismissed in such rapid succession that there was a delay while the next batsman 'padded-up' ready to walk out to the wicket. In the hiatus the batsman at the non-striker's end chatted with the bowler, remarking that their bosses had argued at a meeting that morning. They talked about what a pain it was, realised between them what was actually wanted and what was possible, resolved the issue and had it implemented by the end of the week.

What was different at the match?

- No politics – in terms of concern with image and relative positions of power within the organisation.

- The staff worked at a lower level and knew what was actually required in terms of supporting the business process, and what was possible from the installed IS services and infrastructure.

- They recognised their common goal, and it helped that they liked and wanted to help each other.

If both parties have respect for each other, then progress is possible and with effort can be achieved. If both parties like each other, share common goals and understandings, then success is almost guaranteed.

Perspectives for negotiation

For negotiation, the key Business Perspective issues are:

- remember the purpose
- keep focused, let goals and business requirements drive the process – keep asking 'What does the business need to do its job?'
- involve all parties, not necessarily all at once, but keep an eye on all of them – customers, users and suppliers – including people a step or two away in the supply chain
- there are likely to be other discussions and alliances in place that don't involve you – don't feel you have to be involved in everything, but try to ensure that there are channels that bring you the information you need. Don't underestimate the value of networking.

5.3 Service Catalogue and the Portfolio of Services

One of the most powerful tools for demonstrating and establishing a viable Business Perception is the concept of a service. If the IS (or indeed any other) services are to be delivered and supported in a way that supports the business, then the 'services' considered, delivered and measured must be expressed in terms that are understood by the business. Therefore valid services cannot be identified by anyone armed only with knowledge of the service provider's environment, no matter how complete and available that service provider's knowledge may be.

If services are not expressed in business terms then it will be all but impossible to deliver, and certainly to measure, them in a way that, above all, supports the business needs. There is a long and still healthy tradition of getting this wrong. Popular examples include:

- describing services to match the internal organisational structure of the service provider, e.g. support of C++ or COBOL systems

- matching services to the technological infrastructure, e.g. considering the provision of a LAN or a mainframe as a service

- 'passing on', as services to the customer, supplies bought in from other areas, e.g. treating OLAs and underpinning contracts as the starting point for an SLA.

Instead organisations should seek amongst the customers, and especially the users, what they consider to be a service. It can be argued that there is unlikely to be such a thing as strictly an 'IS service' because:

- almost inevitably in any usable service there is an inherent element that is not IS, e.g. a paper form, a piece of knowledge in an individual's head, an item requiring physical transportation

- users use the IS element of their business support as it suits them, not separately according to supply, so services evolve according to business practice.

Tip

To achieve the necessary Business Perspective, users, as opposed to customers, are a significant source of relevant information. Whatever customers may expect or intend in terms of how services are used and processes deliver business products, in practice the processes and usage evolve almost organically.

This evolution means that services evolve too, and the Service Catalogue must be actively maintained to deliver the benefits it can.

5.3.1 Portfolio of Services

The Service Catalogue is a product of the IS service provider, and it is populated with the IS services that the service provider delivers. These services inevitably have non-IS elements within their functionality, which are those elements necessary to ensure that only the services that can be perceived by the customer as an entity are included. These services are one element of the bigger Portfolio of Services that is made available to the customer. This is the document (real or virtual) setting out the services which:

- are or will be available for use within the business
- are supported by one or more service providers
- can be managed and interpreted by a Business Relationship Manager.

It also includes elements from the Business Change Plan that set out which new services are to be introduced. Where (as is often the case) different component elements of a service are supported by different service providers, then all the different service providers must be involved in creating a single, comprehensive entity in the Portfolio of Services. The alternative is that misleading duplicates or omissions inevitably lead to a less efficient business performance when all the available supporting facilities are not fully known and understood.

The language in which the services are described and the format used for the portfolio are important to ensure that the portfolio is understood and embraced by the business. If an organisation has a business relationship management function, it is likely that they own the Portfolio of Services. As such, they are responsible for liaising with service providers and obtaining appropriate input. The most effective mechanism for conveying the required information is likely to be in the form and style most used within the business. Research to discover the best way to present it, so that it is received and understood, is well worth the effort. Appendix B.3 provides an example of minimum information about a service for inclusion within a Portfolio of Services.

5.4 Informed Customer

Informed Customer (IC) is a term that came into use in the late 1990s to describe a customer with some IS perspective.

Typically the areas of involvement of ICs are:

- the alignment of business and IS plans and strategies
- the development of Business Unit objectives and requirements for IS
- the establishment and co-ordination of user groups
- membership of the ISG and active involvement in the prioritisation of investment, projects and changes
- the development, negotiation and agreement of SLRs and SLAs
- managing the provision of the IS services on behalf of their Business Unit
- selecting the sources of IS service provision and procurement
- ensuring that the services delivered are used effectively to benefit the business and that the business obtains value for money
- the integration of business processes and underpinning IS services
- the education and training of other business personnel in IS issues, services and their usage.

As IS becomes ever more pervasive, and an integral and inseparable part of everyday business, one would expect IS awareness to increase. But that is not to say that the business will bridge the gap between IS and the customer through that knowledge. As IS becomes more sophisticated in what it can do, much effort is going into making it more intuitive to use, and reducing the amount of IS knowledge needed to exploit its possibilities.

Many years ago, those wishing to use cars either developed significant knowledge of automobile mechanics, or employed full-time chauffeur-mechanics. Now very little technical knowledge is required to drive a car. It seems that the IS world is following that precedent, becoming an everyday product to be 'driven' without the need for any technical knowledge.

To facilitate easy and effective delivery of service, the IS service provider needs to ensure the customer knows (and this knowledge is maintained):

- the services they receive, and their importance to the delivery of business outputs
- what to do when the services are not performing as expected, at several levels:
  - incidents, complaints, service requests – contact the Service Desk, with appropriate information
  - changes – input to the Change Management process, knowledge of Requests for Change (RFCs) and rules for submitting, justifying and assessing them
- levels of service – via Service Level Management, or Business Relationship Management.

The waterline concept

For most situations, the businesses do not need to be aware of 'how' an IS service works – rather they need to be familiar with how to get the results and support they need to do their own jobs and deliver against their own (business) targets.

The concept of a waterline can be very helpful in recognising the different types of understanding required by customers and suppliers as depicted in Figure 5.3. Above the waterline are the business-related services that customers and users are familiar with as part of their business procedures. Below the waterline are the mechanics of how the service provider supports the business services.

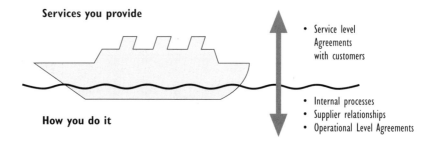

Figure 5.3 – The waterline concept

When there is trust and confidence on the part of the customer, then they have no need to be aware of the details of how the technical components of the service are constructed. The user does not need to understand how IS works – in fact that knowledge is likely to get in the way of using it. The service provider should take responsibility for the internal process, and be judged by the external deliverable.

Example

The magic cupboard

Any suitably advanced technology is indistinguishable from Magic (Arthur C. Clarke)

Users of technology have two ways of treating that technology and incorporating it into their daily lives – to understand how it works, or to treat it as 'magic'. The understanding approach works but is expensive in terms of the amount of unnecessary knowledge and learning required.

Take as a simple example an ordinary domestic washing machine. One could understand all the technology involved: the electric motor, the biochemical reactions by which tomato sauce leaves cotton shirts, the dynamics of the drum rotation, etc. Or you can put dirty clothes into the magic cupboard, add the sacrificial offerings of powder, set the spells on the dials and leave it for two hours. When you return the magic has worked and turned the clothes clean.

In practice, the best path lies between the two extremes, but realising how little needs to be understood of the 'how' in order to get the benefits is a salutary lesson for many technophiles. Even the most avowed 'IS techies' are basing their knowledge on the provision of something they take for granted. After all, all semiconductor technology rests upon sub-atomic quantum probability, but you don't need to fully understand that to use Windows.

5.5 Informed suppliers

The corollary to the concept of an Informed Customer is that suppliers should also be appropriately informed, in terms of their knowledge of the customer's environment. How much does the supplier need to know about the customer's business to understand the Business Perspective? That understanding is likely to include:

- how the service is to be used, both expectation and reality of usage
- how the service will be judged, both by users and customers
- what changes could reasonably be expected in how the service will be required and used
- what the customer is worried about in terms of business imperatives
- how the service provider is going to get relevant information, and keep it up to date
- service level review meetings: their frequency, location, etc. and how seriously they are treated
- Business Relationship Management, either by doing it directly or getting feedback from whoever does it
- contacts and routes to networking and informal discussion with knowledgeable customer staff

■ formal training requirements, e.g. customer staff's induction training

■ business plans, briefings, budgets, priorities

■ Change Advisory Board involvement.

5.6   Communication with Business Customers

Developing and maintaining the appropriate degree of business understanding rests upon meaningful communication between the two parties. This communication takes place at varying levels, reflecting strategic, tactical and operational communications, and accordingly centring on different components of the business and IS communities as shown in Figure 5.4.

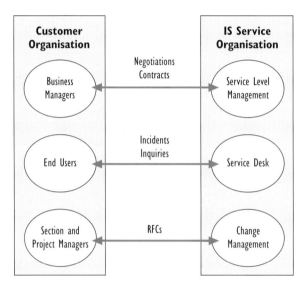

Figure 5.4 – Levels of communication

Whatever level of communication, it needs to be couched in terms that are clearly understood, i.e. they relate to perceivable services being delivered, and using business rather than IS jargon. Any terms capable of being misinterpreted need to be defined in an agreed, readily available and jointly owned glossary.

This is not always as easy to achieve as it sounds, since it requires an understanding of the way the other person thinks and sees the world, which is not a common skill, and one that requires constant effort. Techniques for developing and, crucially, for maintaining this understanding might include:

■ job swaps, visits, awareness of business roles for IS staff

■ frequent joint workshops on development and support of the IS and other services

■ agreement of organisation-wide terminology and acronyms

■ discussing with those who have the knowledge and experience to say how information will be perceived – the customers and users themselves and the Service Desk staff who interact with them.

5.6.1   Service reporting

Attention needs to be paid to the different levels of reports supplied. For example, output from the Balanced Scorecard gives the highest level of information. There is a tendency to provide many low-level data reports, simply because the data is easy to obtain and the tools available to IS are familiar. Typically, the best value to the customer is from something in between, and the precise nature, content and frequency of this reporting needs to be developed and maintained in co-operation with the customer.

5.6.2   Perception of information

ITIL talks about two types of metric to evaluate services:

- external metrics that measure the service as perceived by the customer
- internal metrics used to measure the internal processes that support the business delivery.

Simply quoting numbers does not necessarily convey the same meaning to all, or necessarily even an accurate message, e.g. numbers measured as an average over time may not reflect the customer perspective of a service being critical at some time periods, and unimportant at others.

Example

An organisation implemented a simple prioritisation of incidents based upon numerical levels from 0 to 3, where 0 is the greatest impact. The Service Desk waste considerable time, typically when it can least be spared – during the recording of major incidents – explaining priority zero to customers. Most of them are bemused when told that their concern has been allocated a priority of zero. For most people in business the term 'zero' is associated with unimportance and lack of urgency!

There is a tendency to believe implicitly any numbers that are professionally presented. Failure to appreciate that any expressed numbers are subject to errors of measurement may lead to business decisions based on incorrect risk assessments.

It is not just numbers that are open to misinterpretation. Unless efforts are put into learning and maintaining relevant knowledge, IS are unlikely to understand how factors are interpreted, such as:

- delays in the delivery or updating of services or new features, e.g. delays in the release management process
- unavailability of services, e.g. at specific times and locations which may have special significance to the business
- costs incurred because of IS, such as staff overtime following service interruptions.

5.7   Business continuity

The business community is concerned with their ability to deliver business services under all circumstances, and not necessarily with the replacement of ICT technology. In the event that ICT alone is affected by a disaster, then the ICT replacement may be an appropriate focus. However, if more areas than ICT are affected (e.g. the site is unavailable) then the IS contingency must support the circumstances the business might find itself in.

Example

The Business Continuity Plan addresses how to cope with the loss of an administrative building. A typical response may be to encourage a high percentage of staff to work from home, reserving available administrative accommodation for those whose presence together is essential. This is a procedural reaction to the contingency situation, on the face of it with little direct effect on the IS unit, since the same people are using the same IS services in more or less the same timeframe. However, the impacts and implications of supporting a single location of users accessing a LAN might be very different from the requirements imposed by several hundred users working from home over dial-up or domestic broadband connections. Not only are technical, network implications to be considered, but also people issues such as changes in the numbers and types of call that may be received by the Service Desk.

IT Service Continuity Plans must be derived so as to be flexible enough to support all the contingency options anticipated by the business in their Business Continuity Plans. And where IS is not the only service provider affected, it is necessary to consider how IS support for the other internal service providers may, in turn, be affected.

When it comes to deciding on continuity strategies, the business may well take a different risk-based perspective than that adopted or anticipated by IS. For example, one manufacturing organisation opted to take no action to protect themselves against the loss of their main site. The board accepted that it would be crippling to the business should they lose the site, but felt that the risk was acceptable in exchange for the savings achieved, which made their product more competitive against other suppliers in the same business.

5.8   Future business requirements – getting a strategic view

To deliver the requirements of Business Capacity Management, account must be taken of the business expectations for the future, typically in some detail for the next financial year, and more generally for the next few years.

Merely asking the business and taking the answer at face value may not deliver the required accuracy, and almost certainly not the best level of accuracy possible. The business expresses forecasts in its own way, and these might include:

- exaggerations to impress its customers, creditors, competitors or marketplace
- understatement, typically a sales team may under-predict if their bonus is based upon the degree by which they exceed targets
- use of 'accepted industry measures', e.g. network capabilities are typically expressed as a theoretical maximum, much in excess of what is practically achievable in a real-world installation.

Therefore, to determine as realistic as possible estimates and forecasts of business activities, some 'informed massaging' of the raw data received from the business and related sources is required. To achieve this successfully requires knowledge of the business, and its approach. One simple yet powerful technique is to compare this year's actual figures with those predicted by the business for that year. A good starting point is to apply the same factor of difference to the current predictions. For example, let us suppose that the sales forecast for last year was 20,000 units, but actual sales were 40,000. If the sales team are now predicting 30,000 sales next year, a good starting point for a working figure might be 60,000, i.e. expect both actual figures to be 200% of prediction. It is sensible though, to discuss the situation since other circumstances may have changed and in practice an informal, undocumented and unattributable approach to those predicting figures often gives the best level of information as to the thinking behind business predictions.

5.8.1 Business Impact Analysis

ITIL uses impact as an important element of Incident, Problem and Change Management, and points out that this should be the business impact that is considered. To assess, or at the least discuss meaningfully, degrees of business impact, it is necessary to have some knowledge of the business. The level of actual or potential impact that an incident, problem or change may have on the business can vary according to perceptions. Also, perceptions can vary between departments in the same business, e.g. production, finance or marketing departments.

Within a single business area the impact may vary according to:

- time of the day, week, month or year, e.g. accounts printers on the last day of the month; retail systems in the weeks before Christmas; aircraft navigation systems three metres above the runway

- presence of important people, e.g. visits by the Foreign Secretary to an obscure overseas embassy

- special events, e.g. conference room technology on the day of the AGM.

This awareness relies on establishing good working communications with the business at a strategic level to identify key business elements and risks to them, but also at an operational level to consider the actual impact of each incident or change as it is recorded.

5.8.2 Delivering the business requirements

Considerable documentation exists on a multiplicity of approaches designed to discover and then deliver the business requirement. The *Application Management* book addresses much of the necessary interface between Service Management and Application Development.

Traditionally IS has adopted a procedural approach to specifying and building IS services. There is a need, however, to understand the context in which the requirements exist, and specifically the business requirement as the service is supported, which may well be more dynamic than the initial statement of a service requirement.

The traditional approach of technical supporting services, including IS, is going straight to a suggested solution rather than understanding the question within its business context. Often a technical solution is expected and delivered, concentrating solely on the mechanism of service delivery, instead of how to achieve the service required.

Example

The IS unit of a financial company believed that they had a long-standing issue with excessive network traffic. Considerable money had been spent on highly skilled technical consultancy, which had involved examining network usage statistics and proposing very expensive and high-risk fundamental network changes.

Meanwhile a student, working for a year in industry as part of his degree, and short of tasks to do, was told to go and look at the issue, with the expectation that it would keep him 'quiet for a while', and out of the manager's hair. Instead the student came back next day with the answer. Instead of looking at network logs, the student had sat down with users and seen how they used the major company financial report package.

A few judicious questions elicited the realisation that on-line reports were not essential, but were the default setting in the program. A one-line code change to alter the default, so that reports were produced off-line and emailed to users, resolved the network issue, removed the need for expensive technical reconstruction and satisfied the customers and users.

5.9   Role of Service Level Requirements

Service Level Requirements is the key area where the Business Perspective is fed into the IS delivery. Traditionally IS have put considerable effort into identifying and expressing in IS terms the functional requirements of the business. This approach can be restricting in that:

- by concentrating on the IS interpretation, the full purpose and nature of the service, which is likely to include non-IS elements, is lost to the service provider. Once lost from view, the service cannot be delivered. The Business Perspective, however, requires just that – understanding what the service must do, not what the IS equipment does to deliver its component

- concentrating only on the functional requirements ignores availability, performance, support and other service requirements, without which strict delivery of the functional requirements cannot be turned into actual delivery of those functional requirements to the business

- where Service Level Requirements are not formally considered and documented (even if taken account of), changes to them are not detected and accounted for, and changes to the way the functional requirements are delivered can have a devastating effect on the deliverable levels of service

- while the need for 'non-functional' requirements, which cover availability, performance, etc. is understood, there is also the need to understand how users will use the service. Failure to consider usability requirements can deliver a service that does not deliver business benefit because users cannot 'get it to do what they expect and require'. This may be due to a 'non-user sympathetic' design or not being delivered or supported in a way that facilitates real user benefit.

Example

Once upon a time, many years ago now …

A stock control system was being developed, to introduce on-line ordering, allocation and selecting of goods from warehouses. A prototype version was developed and demonstrated. It wasn't bad, but the users required a change which was technically trivial, as selecting and confirming the total allocated stock wasn't adequate, because each pallet or location used to meet an order needed to be selected and confirmed separately. This was solved with two lines of COBOL. But this multiplied the message pairs travelling over the network by a factor of 12 (as calculated afterwards – after the whole system stopped the day it went live!)

The Service Level Requirement can also extend to establishing and determining how the users will use a service. Failure to understand the user perspective can be expensive, embarrassing and on occasions has proved fatal when developing services. The factors that matter to the business may not be visible or comprehensible to the service provider.

5.10 Business change: mergers, acquisitions and reorganisation

This kind of significant business change is going to have knock-on significant changes to the IS requirements. In these circumstances the actions are driven by business imperatives, sometimes resulting in IS being overlooked until the later stages. There are examples of high profile business changes coming unstuck because the technology was unable to support the new shape of the organisation.

People's view of where the problem lies stems from the differing perspectives that exist – from the business it is an IS inadequacy, from IS it is the business's ignorance of what is possible.

The truth lies between the two extremes, or perhaps it is in the inability of either or both parties to talk meaningfully with each other. This is an excellent example of the need for communication in both directions, and with enough common understanding to make the communication meaningful.

The most obvious method for driving this appropriate level of communication is via the project and programme management disciplines within an organisation.

6 MANAGING THE PROVISION OF SERVICE

The service provider is responsible for providing IS services to the business, from the initial gathering of business requirements through application development, service deployment, day-to-day management, continuous improvement, and eventual retirement. For the business to view these services as being successful, they need to be of high quality, must meet changing business requirements, and be provided at an appropriate cost.

To achieve these goals, the service provider must have a clear understanding of business requirements and a mature IT Service Management implementation. The ITIL publications identified in Figure 1.1 provide significant guidance in this respect and help a service provider identify and respond to the needs of the business. The Business Perspective approach discussed in this book describes the need for even greater alignment between IS and the business, with the ultimate goal of IS being seen by the business as an innovator and enabler of new business opportunity and capability, and not simply as a reliable provider of existing functionality.

From the service provider's viewpoint, reliability, efficiency, effectiveness and maturity can be achieved through the implementation of best practice and good governance, and through the achievement of appropriate industry certifications such as ISO 9000 quality and BS 15000 IT Service Management.

Closer business alignment almost certainly emerges from such activities, but there also needs to be a specific strategic push in this respect and an overall culture needs to be built focused on the business as outlined in Chapters 4 and 5. From the Business Perspective, the impact of this culture on the ITIL processes themselves is often to extend their scope further towards the business with, for example, the IS Change Management process being much more closely integrated with the wider business change processes.

Therefore, closer business alignment is not just the domain of the *Business Perspective* book, but a business-focused approach which needs to be applied across all processes within the core ITIL publications as shown in Figure 6.1 and, where of benefit, extended into the business.

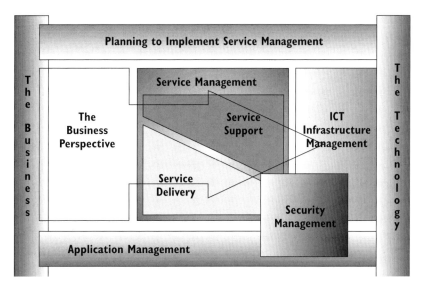

Figure 6.1 – The Business Perspective being applied

Earlier chapters of this book have made the case for closer business alignment, the benefits that can be derived, and the approaches that can be taken. But what does closer business alignment look like? How should we shape our processes and what difference will it make to our interfaces and day-to-day activities? This chapter brings together existing business alignment best practice contained within the above ITIL publications and develops it further, helping to explain how the service provider can engage effectively with the business and giving specific examples of well-aligned processes. The content is designed to be of benefit to both new and seasoned users of ITIL, acting as a focal point for existing best practice whilst providing new insight and greater depth.

The remainder of this chapter is broken into the following major themes:

- ITIL process integration
- new services
- service reporting
- education.

ITIL process integration discusses closer process alignment from the point of view of both the service provider and the business, and identifies how such alignment can be achieved in practice. Section 6.2 on new services examines the considerations of expanding the service provider's Portfolio of Services, and Section 6.3 on service reporting looks at how the service provider can best represent its deliverables to the business. Section 6.4 on education considers the training and awareness required to underpin a Business Perspective approach in IS.

6.1   ITIL process integration

Starting with Service Delivery and Service Support, the following sections discuss each of the core ITIL publications and the processes they contain from the Business Perspective, and identify how the service provider can achieve closer alignment with the business.

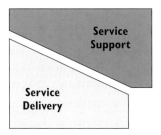

6.1.1   Service Desk

The Service Desk function is the place where the service provider comes into the closest and most frequent contact with the users of IS services. The service provider thus has the opportunity to shape both its own image and also the image of the business as seen by the consumers of IS services, and the opportunity needs to be taken to present a very professional and responsive service through the Service Desk function.

By working closely with the business, the Service Desk can offer to extend its reach from purely IS service-related activities to business process-related activities such as conference room bookings, facilities requests, product usage support, voice and telephone support, management reporting, satisfaction surveys, complaints handling, etc.

Where it makes sense for the organisation, the Service Desk can increasingly become a front-end for the business as well as for the service provider. This places the Service Desk in a position to help the business identify new business opportunities by engaging in dialogue with the end-user around product weaknesses, usage issues, and by soliciting feedback.

The interpersonal skills of Service Desk staff is a key element in their success and they need to be trained in the needs of the business and have a strong understanding, in business terms, of the importance of the services they support. This understanding then shapes everything they do.

To achieve improved Service Desk process integration, the service provider and the business should adopt the following approach:

- the business views the Service Desk as an extension of its own business processes and as a valuable means of managing the needs of their users – and not just a point of contact for technology and IS service-related problems

- the range of services provided by the Service Desk includes business-process-related activities such as the dissemination of information as well as IS service support activities such as incident handling

- the Service Desk staff and processes focus on achieving high levels of customer satisfaction and achieving a positive perception by the business and user communities

- interaction with the business and users is personalised as often as possible with each interaction advising of the next steps that can be expected and providing details of where to go for more information or clarification

- the Service Desk services are easy to use and the consistency and quality of the support they provide encourages users to come back for more and build trust in their capabilities

- second-level support staff are involved in Service Desk activities either routinely or on a rotational basis – the Service Desk benefits from access to appropriate resource when required, and the second-level support groups benefit from an increased understanding of the needs of the business and the real-world challenges faced by their users

- the Service Desk provides proactive management information, including recommendations for service improvement, and identification of any need for user training and education.

6.1.2   Incident Management and Problem Management

Incident Management and Problem Management have a key role to play in the resolution of service incidents and the identification, mitigation and correction of errors in the underlying infrastructure and processes. Shortcomings and opportunities for improvement in business products and business processes can also be visible at this level, and in addition to the natural interface and feedback provided to IS developers, the Incident and Problem Management processes can also be extended right back to the wider product development, marketing, and user training processes within the business organisation.

There is often an understandable contention between the approach of the business and the approach of the service provider when it comes to handling service-affecting incidents.

Example

A major system failure resulted in data being corrupted during a number, but not all, of subsequent business transactions.

The service provider's approach was to take the service off-line, fix the code, recover data integrity and then restore the service. Any continuance of the service in its current state would only compound the data corruption and extend any subsequent recovery. This approach would take the whole service down for several hours.

However, the business's perspective was that they would rather carry on as they were – the majority of transactions were functioning and they would be happy to delay recovery of the complete system until the weekend when they would be happy to lose the whole system for an extended period, despite the risk and likelihood of further data corruptions occurring.

The business needs to own such decision-making once they have been made aware of the complete picture.

To achieve improved Incident and Problem Management integration, the service provider and the business should adopt the following approach:

- the business must be involved when the Incident and Problem Management processes are being designed to ensure that:
  - incident categories and priorities are appropriate for accurately determining the business impact and identifying an appropriate response
  - the processes are able to meet business-required timescales for response, update and resolution
  - the type and amount of data that users are required to submit during incident logging are acceptable to the user community and do not unduly hinder their normal work nor require them to learn unnecessary technical jargon
  - appropriate criteria have been identified to determine when the time required for the collection of data for root cause analysis can take precedence over the speed of service restoration
  - the escalation process is compatible with the business escalation process and ties in at the appropriate points to meet business requirements effectively
  - reports from the Incident and Problem Management processes are couched in business terminology and identify the value being delivered to the business and do not just reflect internal service provider metrics

- the business and IS work together to provide:
  - ongoing training for users to ensure that they know how to log incidents in the most efficient manner and have appropriate expectations of the response they will receive
  - regular review of report content and structure to ensure these continue to meet business needs.

6.1.3 Configuration Management

Although not as obvious as some of the other Service Management processes, a closer business alignment around Configuration Management is also beneficial to the service provider and the business, and can lead to greater efficiency in other processes such as Incident, Problem and Change Management. Configuration Management is also similar to the wider Business Asset Management process and benefits can be derived from a more formal linkage between the two.

To achieve improved Configuration Management integration, the service provider and the business should adopt the following approach:

- the service provider's overall configuration management design includes formal involvement from the business:
  - the level of detail to be stored about each Configuration Item (CI) is agreed so that both the business and service provider can obtain the data and reports they need
  - appropriate feeds between configuration data and existing business and asset data are identified so that information about people, buildings, and other non-IT assets can be included as appropriate to increase environmental knowledge at the time of user interaction and to reduce duplication
  - audit processes are aligned so that efficiency savings can be achieved by combining IS configuration audits with other business audits or asset checks

- the Service Level Agreements specify that all communication about incidents, changes, service continuity or other aspects of the service are based on clear and unambiguous usage of CI names, and where relevant that these naming conventions match those employed by the business

- advantage is taken during the incident logging process to verify the accuracy of configuration data in a routine non-intrusive fashion that helps identify errors and improve the quality of future user interactions.

Example

A conversation between a Service Desk operative and user:

'Good morning Mr Smith, thank you for logging your enquiry with us. Can I just confirm with you that you are normally located in Building 3 and your PC is an Armada 700 laptop?'

'I am not in Building 3 any more. We moved to Building 2 over six months ago.'

6.1.4 Change Management

The service provider's Change Management processes are responsible for the efficient and controlled implementation of all changes to live IS services and supporting ICT infrastructure, with changes either arising reactively in response to service incidents, or proactively to implement improved business functionality or improvements in Service Management processes.

Businesses also need to manage change effectively to remain attractive to their customers and to remain competitive in the marketplace or respond to legislative changes. As businesses are increasingly dependent on IS services for their day-to-day operation, such business change often needs to be enabled by IS.

There are also other drivers for business change, including technology developments, cost-effectiveness and continuous improvements. As such, it is part of the service provider's responsibility to bring these to the attention of the business and to explain the potential business benefits, allowing the service provider to be considered part of the wider business research and development efforts.

As can be seen, it is increasingly important for the IS Change Management process to be closely integrated with the wider business Change Management processes.

To achieve improved Change Management integration, the service provider and the business should adopt the following approach:

- The service provider's overall Change Management process specifically includes formal involvement from the business throughout the entire life cycle:
  - the Change Advisory Board (CAB) includes senior business and user representation
  - all changes are authorised and prioritised by the business either directly or through agreed categories of change that are effectively pre-authorised
  - the business impact of change on Service Level Agreements and IT Service Continuity commitments is carefully assessed
  - where the CAB cannot come to an agreement, or the impact and resource requirements are beyond its scope to authorise, the Change Management process passes responsibility to a higher authority such as the IS director who liaises with correspondingly senior business representatives
  - emergency change and standard change procedures specifically address when business approval is required, and when it is not

- implementation timescales are based upon and work around business timelines and not service provider timelines

- a Forward Schedule of Change is maintained summarising all approved changes and their implementation details, and made available widely within the business and user communities

- regular planned maintenance slots are negotiated between the service provider and the business and these provide sufficient time to ensure that the rate of change required by the business can be accommodated by IS

- all changes, whether successful or unsuccessful, are subject to post-implementation review from both the technical and business perspectives – by reviewing change together, the shared knowledge and joint learning leads to improvements in relationships and more successful change in future
  - Was the outcome as expected?
  - Have the expected business benefits been realised?
  - Are there any lessons that can be learned?

- the wider business change processes include formal involvement from the service provider:
  - business product development and existing product review exercises include senior service provider representation so that appropriate technology options and issues can be considered at the most appropriate stage in the life cycle

–   the service provider takes part in future business product research activities and the evaluation of the business's customer satisfaction surveys.

6.1.5   Release Management

Release Management is responsible for the implementation of new or changed hardware and software components into the production environment. A large part of the benefit to be derived from a close business alignment will already have been derived through other management process interactions during earlier stages of the identification and authorisation of planned changes and associated releases. Release Management itself also needs to ensure that the business is appropriately consulted and kept informed during the work it undertakes.

To achieve improved Release Management integration, the service provider and the business should adopt the following approach:

■   the service provider's Release Management process specifically includes formal involvement from the business

■   the business appreciates the need for infrastructure upgrades and 'technology' releases even though they do not have any obvious business benefit – such releases and how they add value to be included within an ongoing education programme (see Service Level Management in Section 6.1.6)

■   the business and IS define an appropriate Release Policy to suit individual situations while being as cost-effective as possible

■   the content of each release is prioritised and agreed by the business

■   a planned release schedule is maintained summarising all approved releases and their implementation details, and made available widely within the business and user community

■   release schedules are based on and work around business timelines and not service provider timelines

■   all releases, whether successful or unsuccessful, are subject to post-implementation review from both the technical and business perspectives – by reviewing releases together, shared knowledge and joint learning leads to improvements in relationships and more successful releases in future

■   overall business change planning includes consideration of the need for integrated releases:
    –   the service provider is involved as early as possible in plans that could possibly require co-ordinated releases
    –   potential conflicts between the release requirements of different parts of the business are managed to ensure best overall value and benefit to the business.

6.1.6   Service Level Management

The Service Level Management (SLM) process forms a crucial link between the service provider and the business. To manage its responsibilities effectively, SLM develops and manages Service Level Agreements (SLAs) with the Business, Operational Level Agreements (OLAs) with internal organisations, and Underpinning Contracts (UCs) with third party suppliers. As a minimum, it is essential that the business is closely involved in the development of SLAs and associated targets and that these commitments can be achieved by the service provider cost-effectively.

The business is also engaged in very similar activities with the commitments it makes to its own Business Customers and the contracts it has with internal and external suppliers. Recognising this synergy, and the benefits that can be derived from close alignment between the service provider and the business, the Business Perspective approach works to combine these activities so that the service provider's SLM process is seen as a key component of the bigger business SLM process.

In this way, the earliest requirements from the Business Customers and end-users regarding new or changed products and services to be supplied by the business, and the commitments being made by the business in response, are visible to the service provider. This allows any implications on the service provider to be fed into the process right from the beginning. The service provider also has an excellent opportunity to explain to the business and its customers the benefits that can be derived from advances in technology and starts to be seen as an enabler of opportunity and a true business partner.

SLM is therefore a key process in the Business Perspective approach and many of the roles, tools and techniques deployed within the Business Perspective involve SLM on a day-to-day basis. The Business Relationship Management and Supplier Relationship Management roles are a deepening of the role performed by the Service Level Manager (these roles are defined in Chapter 8). The Service Catalogue maintained by SLM is broadened into a 'Portfolio of Services' and used to market the service provider and its capabilities to all areas of the business.

Example

A number of cheque printers had no service contract and were not considered part of the overall IS service – until they went wrong at month end!

To achieve improved Service Level Management integration, the service provider and the business should adopt the following approach:

- the service provider's SLM process includes formal involvement from the business with regular participation from senior business personnel across the full life cycle
- an ongoing education programme is put in place to ensure both parties have a sound understanding of each other: to educate the business about the nature of IS that supports them; and to educate the service provider about the needs of the business they support
- IS services are designed around the true business need and in pursuit of realistic and achievable business requirements
- SLAs are expressed in business terms and in language that is clearly understood by both parties
- the SLM process is closely integrated with the wider Business Relationship Management role
- Key Performance Indicators (KPIs) and service reporting includes metrics of direct relevance to the business
- formal customer satisfaction surveys are undertaken on a regular basis to gauge the satisfaction of the business and user communities and the service provider is involved in the evaluation of the business's own customer satisfaction surveys
- the business has senior representation on the Service Improvement steering group to

help position the benefits to be gained from potential improvement activities against existing commitments and the demands of new business functionality

- the wider business SLM-like processes include formal involvement from the service provider:
  - business product and process management activities include senior service provider representatives so that appropriate technology options and issues can be considered and appropriate expectations set at the most appropriate stage in the life cycle
  - the service provider takes part in future business product/process research activities.

6.1.7 Availability Management and IT Service Continuity Management

Availability Management and IT Service Continuity Management (ITSCM) work together to ensure that the agreed IS services are available when and where they are required and both of these activities clearly need to be closely aligned with the business so that the impact of downtime can be properly assessed and appropriate countermeasures designed within the available budget. However, close integration is also required with the overall Business Continuity Management (BCM) role within the organisation.

BCM is responsible for ensuring that the organisation and its key business processes can continue to function in the event of disaster and that an acceptable level of service can still be provided to its customers and internal functions. The *PAS 56 Guide to Business Continuity Management* has further details on best practice guidance on BCM from the British Standards Institution (BSi) and the Business Continuity Institute (BCI).

The continuity of IS services is a key concern for BCM. ITSCM therefore needs to be a formal part of the overall BCM process. ITSCM needs to be driven by BCM and the business requirements for a particular service established in conjunction with BCM, and driven by the initial risk assessment.

Example

An important business workflow model running on a stand-alone PC was identified, about which IS had no knowledge. The PC and its data were not secure nor were they backed up. Such issues will be identified as the business and IS work closer together.

To achieve improved Availability and IT Service Continuity Management integration, the service provider and the business should adopt the following approach:

- the service provider's Availability and IT Service Continuity Management processes includes regular formal involvement from senior business personnel
- the service provider and the business work together to produce co-ordinated Business Impact Analysis and risk assessment of business and IS services
- critical business processes that are supported by IS services and ICT infrastructure are identified
- a Business Impact Analysis and risk assessment are undertaken on each IS service or infrastructure component supporting business-critical processes

- the cost of unavailability or service outage is documented and the levels of availability and service continuity deployed by the service provider and the cost implications are formally agreed with the business

- the business has appropriate expectations of the availability that can be realised from their IS services within the cost constraints they have imposed, and so long as the service provider performs as expected during times of service failure, customer satisfaction can still remain high

- the business has agreed the recovery point objectives and recovery time objectives for its IS services

- the service provider's Change Management process, and the wider business change processes include formal sign-off that the impact on Availability Management and ITSCM have been fully considered before any changes are approved

- the wider Business Continuity Management process includes formal involvement from the service provider

  - the service provider's IT Service Continuity Management process is a formal part of the wider Business Continuity Management process
  - ITSCM feeds BCM with risk and countermeasure data so that appropriate impact and cost benefit analysis can be undertaken
  - regularly tested IT Service Continuity plans are in place and appropriately integrated with wider BCM plans
  - business continuity and IT service continuity testing are co-ordinated where appropriate and both parties seek to learn from each other.

See also the discussion of Business Impact Analysis within Section 7.5.6.

6.1.8 Financial Management for IT services

Financial Management for IT services is responsible for the management of Budgeting, Accounting and Charging for Services, and is invariably overseen by the organisation's overall Finance department. As a result, a large part of the benefit to be derived from a close business alignment is already achieved through natural integration and business control. However, this financial linkage needs to be more than just one of the standardised accounting practices and there needs to be a genuine alignment and understanding between the service provider and the business around the true cost of any demands made on the service provider and the limitations of technology and the implications of legacy systems and ageing technology.

In return, the service provider needs to ensure that any services are provided cost-effectively and that the business is receiving value for money. Chapter 4 includes a discussion of Financial Management and the Business Perspective, including Total Cost of Ownership and Return on Investment.

6.1.9 Capacity Management

Capacity planners need to work closely with business planners to gain an understanding of priorities, workloads, throughputs, etc. Capacity Management aims to balance supply and demand cost-effectively, and therefore needs to gain insight from the business into areas where improvements could bring greater business benefits. Business management needs to be able to provide forecasts and plans, focusing on areas of growth or decline, so that capacity planners can ensure that there is sufficient infrastructure capacity and resources to meet their demands. Capacity planners and business planners need to work together to negotiate demand management strategies, such as charging by time of day or excluding some user groups from access to particular functions.

To remain cost-effective and efficient, capacity planners also need to consider areas of growth, decline or consolidation, and work with the business to identify changing product or market trends that can mean resources and infrastructure can be redeployed or disposed of.

The service provider therefore needs to develop a two-way relationship with the business strategy and planning processes within an organisation. They need to understand the long-term strategy of the business while providing information on the latest ideas, trends and technologies being developed by the suppliers of ICT hardware and software.

To achieve improved Capacity Management integration, the service provider and the business should adopt the following approach:

- the service provider's overall Capacity Management process includes regular formal involvement from senior business personnel

- updated business forecasts are provided to the service provider on a regular basis

- updated capacity plans are provided to the business on a regular basis – these plans are discussed and agreed or amended as appropriate

- reports comparing planned and actual capacity and workload are provided to the business on a regular basis

- a formal joint escalation process involving both the business and the service provider is in place to resolve issues caused by inaccurate forecasting

- regular minuted meetings between senior business personnel and the service provider's Capacity Management personnel helps to ensure that information about new technologies is available where this could be of value to the business

- Capacity Management works closely with procurement personnel to help ensure that future requirements are considered in negotiating prices.

6.1.10 Application Management

> **Application Management**

Businesses need to be able to respond rapidly to a changing marketplace, and the service provider is often central to enabling this change. Key to this dilemma is effective management of the applications that are necessary to move the business forward. This is compounded by Internet technology, where Business Customers have direct access and so visibility of the business's ICT. Therefore, the service provider needs to focus on business requirements rather than technology to ensure the most appropriate technology is deployed, as this is enabling business-critical functionality.

The business is interested in Application Management for three primary reasons:

- **financial**: the cost of IS is often seen as huge, with investment in new application functionality seen as delivering business benefit, whilst the cost of operational running is often seen as an overhead. Yet maintenance and support of an application may account for two-thirds of the overall cost of each application during its service life

- **opportunity exploitation**: existing applications can act as a constraint or have an adverse effect on an organisation's ability to exploit new business opportunities and emerging markets

- **quality**: there is a need to address the quality of applications as an integral part of an IS service, especially when the business is critically dependent upon them.

From the Business Perspective, an organisation is keen to obtain application services that reduce customer risk, provide value for money, and give the business a higher degree of freedom in which to exploit opportunities.

As described in Chapter 4, strategic business alignment in the delivery and support of applications is very important to the success of the service provider. However, the applications themselves deliver business functionality to the business on a day-to-day basis, making it essential that the business/IS alignment around that functionality is accurate and ensures that business needs are fully satisfied.

Once these business/IS-aligned applications are deployed, consideration must be given to their management, maximising the investment through long-term effective and ongoing maintainability (i.e. responsive to change and recoverability). Also, their business value does not remain static. An Application Portfolio, as described in Chapter 3 of the *Application Management* book, provides a mechanism for viewing and evaluating the entire suite of applications in the business enterprise, which can be used in combination with the business strategy to develop long-term management strategies for each application.

A key aspect is the definition of ownership of applications within the business, identifying authority to change and/or responsibility for budget. Depending on the breadth of the application usage, ownership may be business function level or business process level, or higher based on the most significant usage across a range of business processes.

Important though applications are in the delivery of business functionality, they are only a piece of the overall business process they serve. The Business Perspective approach to Application Management takes the concept of business alignment a stage further and makes the linkage with business product development and deployment, where the impact of new or changed business functionality has involvement from the service provider at the earliest possible stage.

The service provider should strive to become part of the business product development life cycle and not just the application development life cycle. Once this linkage has been made it needs to be maintained throughout the life cycle of the most significant business function that the application is contributing towards.

The following sections consider the Business Perspective approach within the main phases of an application's life cycle.

Requirements

In this phase in the life cycle, the requirements for a new application are gathered, based on the business needs of the organisation. To undertake this activity, the service provider needs to have good engagement with the relevant business function, including:

- clarity and familiarity with the business language in use

- clear definition and understanding of the business drivers and objectives for this new application

- awareness of any business constraints, e.g. budget or delivery timescales which may override standard IS quality policies and practices

- an understanding of where this applications requirement fits into any larger business product development life cycle

- an understanding of the critical success factors for the business and acceptance testing strategy and criteria.

The business must input its functional, non-functional and usability requirements, and needs to be able to articulate these requirements in its own terms. IS need to provide support to the business to enable them to determine and articulate their needs comprehensively and then be able to translate these business requirements into IS specifications, including SLRs.

Whilst IS is a service provider to the business, to maximise the effectiveness of this activity, those involved need to work in partnership rather than a traditional customer/supplier relationship, since ultimately they both have the same objective of enabling effective and efficient delivery of business requirements and so benefit.

This requirements phase is key, since it defines what subsequent Application Management phases will deliver, and the level of business involvement beyond requirements is limited until the end of the build phase. Thus the consequences of any misunderstandings or poor requirements may not become visible until much later at which time it can be costly to correct.

Design

In this phase, requirements are translated into feature specifications. The goal for application design is satisfying the organisation's requirements, including both the design of the application itself, and the design of the operational model that the application has to run on. This phase is largely internal to IS with limited business involvement although any design issues that arise in trying to satisfy business requirements need to be formally discussed and resolved with the business, so that any inappropriate expectations are ironed out at the earliest opportunity.

Build

In the build phase, both the application and the operational model are made ready for deployment. Application components are coded or acquired, integrated and tested. From the business's perspective, acceptance testing is often the first opportunity for the business to view its new application since the requirements were specified. The purpose of acceptance testing is to verify the application against the business requirements and to give confidence that it is fit for purpose, including SLRs and SLAs.

To achieve improved integration, the service provider and the business should adopt the following approach:

- from the business's perspective, it is important to:
  - have agreed levels of applications development support during acceptance testing to set expectations of both the business testers and IS supporters (e.g. a mini SLA) to include such aspects as hours of cover, responsiveness of support to queries, errors, fixes

- have agreed the release strategy during acceptance testing, both for major and minor defect corrections (such as Release Management)
- have defined acceptance testing processes, including interfaces with IS, e.g. how defects or queries are communicated via a single point of contact, monitoring progress and closure (such as Incident Management)
- have the appropriate level and capability of resource to undertake the acceptance testing

■ for service providers it is important to:

- keep the business involved during application build to avoid any unexpected surprises when acceptance testing takes place and the solution is seen for the first time
- ensure the overall quality of the application delivered into acceptance testing is robust, since this starts to set business perceptions about the quality, reliability and usability of the system, even before it goes live
- deliver a solid and robust test facility in line with business requirements
- understand where the application acceptance test fits into any overall business product development testing activity, which may include process, technology, organisation, training and documentation
- have good IS processes at all touch points with the business during acceptance testing (like a micro support service), e.g. capturing and categorising of test defects, progress updates, reporting, release/fix notifications – these processes need to be integrated with those of the acceptance testing for both efficiency and effectiveness
- provide that the agreed and appropriate level and capability of resource for support and data/environment management is available
- ensure the quality of the query and defect resolutions, and processes provided, since this will set business perceptions for the future live IS service.

Service providers may also be required to provide or deliver training material to the business for any new applications. It is key that this training be set in a business context using business terminology. Depending on the level of training required in the business and the ongoing training needs, service providers may either deliver the training direct or train a 'trainer'. For this role, service providers need strong communication skills and a detailed understanding of the business context or process to be able to deliver a credible performance. An effective way to achieve this is to develop and/or deliver the training in partnership with a business 'champion'.

Deploy

In this phase, both the operational model and the application are deployed. The operational model is incorporated in the existing ICT environment and the application is installed on top of the operational model, using the deployment processes described within the *ICT Infrastructure Management* book and in Section 6.1.12.

Operate

In the operate phase, IS delivers the service required by the business in line with the defined business requirements e.g. SLAs. The Business Perspective approach to this is discussed earlier in this section and in Section 6.1.12.

Optimise

In the optimise phase, the results of the service level performance measurements are analysed and acted upon. Possible improvements are discussed and developments initiated if necessary. The two main strategies in this phase are to maintain and/or improve the service levels and to lower cost. This could lead to another iteration of the applications life cycle or to justifying the retirement of an application.

To achieve improved integration when retiring an application, the service provider and the business should adopt the following approach:

- from the business's perspective, it is important to:
  - define the functionality no longer required or being replaced
  - define and specify the data which can be discarded and the data that needs to be archived or migrated, and the required timeframes
- for service providers, it is important to:
  - have business confirmation of the requirement or viability of application retirement
  - understand and establish appropriate methods of access to archived data for legal or business reasons, depending on the volumes/cost of storage and the type and frequency of access required by the business
  - assess and articulate to the business any impact on other applications and IS services (both due to the retirement of an application and for any ongoing support of archived data systems), and any actions required.

6.1.11 Security Management

Security Management is responsible for protecting the service and its component parts from unauthorised access or interference and for ensuring the confidentiality, integrity and availability of services and data.

The wider business security policies need to be clearly underpinned by sufficient IS security controls to assure:

- **information security**: collecting, storing, handling, processing, and making available, the data upon which the information is based. Safeguarding the confidentiality, integrity and availability of the organisation's information assets

- **infrastructure security**: implementing security controls to handle identified threats or real incidents. Putting in place prevention and reduction, detection and repression, along with correction and recovery controls.

Control

Being responsible for organising and directing the Security Management process itself, this area of activity benefits from business input into the management framework: detailing how security policies and plans are established, implemented, evaluated, maintained and reported on.

A clear understanding of the security risks of the business and the business value of the information and other assets within its Information Systems can only come from a business-led risk assessment and Risk Management strategy.

Following the risk assessments, the creation of a joint business and IS forum to deal with the security of information helps to generate the commitment, direction and accountability necessary to drive effective security controls balanced against value to the business and risk vulnerability.

Plan

In developing the security aspects of SLAs, the service provider needs to work with the business to help them define appropriate business processes requirements with respect to confidentiality, integrity and availability. These form a solid foundation of service level requirements for IS security. Such requirements need to be aligned to, or lead future investment in, IS's security capability.

A Security Plan is used by IS to allocate the responsibility for fulfilling the obligations that are held within the SLAs, which becomes auditable by the business.

Implement

Whilst IS are responsible for implementing the whole range of security controls in response to the security requirements detailed within SLAs, the attitudes and behaviour of people involved in applying them is vital to their success.

Awareness within the business of the need for security controls and their personal responsibility in assuring conformance greatly increases the likelihood of successful implementations, and reduces the risk vulnerabilities.

It is imperative that the business is abreast of all security breaches, and that they are updated at regular intervals regarding resolution progress. Most security breaches justify major incident style management and post 'event' reviews. Those breaches resulting in disciplinary action require significant investment of time and resource within the business in the support and execution of such action, and the impact to business processes also needs to be considered.

Evaluate

During times of internal and external audits not only are the security controls subject to scrutiny but also the adherence to policy and awareness within IS and the business. It is crucial that the business is armed with sufficient knowledge of security policies and controls and their responsibilities.

Communication and training in these areas need to be provided with formal signatory confirmation being sought from all employees that they are aware of their responsibilities with regards to information and infrastructure security.

Maintain

A joint security forum oversees the maintenance of security controls and documentation in the light of the results of periodic reviews, awareness of the changing risk picture, changes in the organisation's security policy and standards, and changes to SLAs.

6.1.12 ICT Infrastructure Management

ICT Infrastructure Management aims to provide a stable ICT and communications infrastructure, and whilst truly technology-focused, it still needs to understand and apply the Business Perspective approach.

In recognition of this the business and IS need to form a joint co-ordinating body, consisting of senior management representatives from various business areas and IS (an IS Steering Group or ISG), with the sole purpose of reviewing both the business and IS plans and strategies to ensure alignment.

ICT design and planning

The design and planning processes within a service provider are concerned with providing overall guidelines for the development and installation of an ICT infrastructure that satisfies the needs of all aspects of the business. It involves the development and maintenance of IS strategies for the deployment of infrastructure solutions to meet business needs.

An effective design and planning process is dependent on input from business planners to develop appropriate IS plans and strategies, to ensure well understood business needs and an ICT infrastructure that serves the business, its products and services. Such alignment needs to be balanced between innovation, risk and cost and may be constrained by the characteristics of the services and systems owned by the business it is supporting.

Joint business cases need to be built by the business and IS with regards to gaining financial approval. These must relate costs to business benefits and cannot be done in isolation. Subsequent ICT plans and projects need continuous involvement of the business and must recognise business-dictated timescales where these are the driving factor.

ICT deployment process

The deployment process within an organisation is concerned with the implementation and rollout of the ICT infrastructure as designed and planned. Deployments are often undertaken using a project life cycle, in which the project team starts with a plan specifying the scope of the deployment, the resource requirements and a time schedule for the deployment of the ICT infrastructure components.

The business has specific responsibilities in relation to deployment, e.g. representation of the customer as a Project Board member, Project Sponsor, and for customer acceptance of the solution. They must work closely with Design and Planning, and deployment must be in terms of standards and methods to be applied. These may be referenced in the contractual terms and conditions.

The business must also be concerned with the effects that the deployment may have on the organisation and its personnel. It is often the case that when new or modified technology solutions are being deployed, it is necessary to consider the changes within the organisation, in terms of business ownership of applications and data, changes to business processes, organisational structure or organisational behaviour, and this needs to be managed carefully, as part of the overall deployment from the Business Perspective.

ICT operations and technical support

The Operations function includes the day-to-day running of computer installations, network services management (i.e. the planning and ongoing management of the communication networks), and systems management to ensure effective operational management of the ICT infrastructure, including the necessary measurement and monitoring, housekeeping and maintenance of the infrastructure.

The Operations function provides the basis for a stable and secure ICT capability on which to provide IS services.

From the Business Perspective, Operations may appear to be technology-focused, but the service aspects must not be ignored, in that effective Operations Management assures the stability of the ICT infrastructure through the definition and application of operability standards, and business-focused monitoring thresholds.

The essential nature of Operations in support of the business must be recognised by both the business and the service provider, particularly in situations that dictate the need for a continuous process, covering 24 hours, 365 days a year.

Whilst the nature of the Operations role is fundamentally technologically driven, the customer experience is greatly improved when ICT Operations have a clear understanding of the technology from a Business Perspective. Knowing what a particular monitored job does for the business, why it runs at that time, the impact of failure on the business, the chain of events that failures instigate, and how a business process spans multiple ICT infrastructure elements and the information flows between them, facilitates a more business-focused approach to impact assessments and resolutions.

6.2   New services

6.2.1   Prerequisites for new services

To protect existing services effectively for the business within the operational environment, any new service must be able to demonstrate conformation to the requirements of the operational arena prior to 'go-live'.

Instrumentation/alerting capabilities

New systems must be able to communicate effectively with Operational Management systems via built-in alerting capabilities. These need particularly to address business-critical aspects of systems to ensure maximum information and efficiency when resolving incidents.

Integration with existing systems

The impact of new systems on existing services and ITSM infrastructure must be considered, including capacity requirements (CPU, storage, I/O), monitoring requirements, skills requirements, etc. Delivery of existing services to the business must not be compromised by new services. Also the business needs to define relative priorities of new services, alongside existing services to provide guidance for resource prioritisation during operational and support activities.

Service hours

Service availability requirements must be agreed and documented between the business and IS via an SLA. Where these hours vary from the existing service provision, any additional costs of service provision need to have been discussed, cost-justified on a business basis and agreed with the business.

Error handling

Known Error situations are documented with full business impact identified, error handling instructions (both technical and business process) and details of any plans to address the error.

Backup/recovery/maintenance

Details of system backup requirements must be provided. These include backup schedules, alongside media requirements and expected duration, to support business continuity requirements from report re-creation, batch failure, on-line system unavailability, system rollback through to full disaster recovery. Understanding the business requirements from the outset means that appropriate recovery can be built into processing, e.g. sufficient checkpoints to allow recovery restarts with minimum impact on overall processing time and therefore delivery of business processes to schedule.

Support arrangements

Support capability must be in place prior to go-live. Alongside technical capability, the support team also need business awareness, especially in the early days of a new service when service confidence and initial impressions are formed.

Operational Acceptance Testing

Operational Acceptance Testing (OAT) must be carried out for all new services prior to go-live. However well-planned an implementation is, without testing in a 'real world' environment it is virtually impossible to identify all those 'touch points' where the new systems may interact with existing systems. After all, who wants to explain to the CEO that his or her email system was unavailable because the (apparently unrelated) new system wasn't thoroughly tested?

6.2.2   Managing business expectations

IS involvement in the decision-making process

The service provider needs to be involved at the very beginning of the decision-making process. Far too frequently, business users identify a need for a new IS service and begin to develop the technical solution in isolation. With limited technical knowledge and even less understanding of the intricacies of the existing infrastructure, this approach invariably leads to conflict with the service provider. Not only can there be difficulties due to incompatibility with existing systems, but it can also force service providers into accepting new services which they are ill-equipped to manage. If the business can involve the service provider as soon as a new business requirement is identified, it is possible for these issues to be minimised leading to a far more successful development process and greatly improving the likelihood of a successful implementation and subsequent live running.

Timescales for implementation

When considering potential threats to the successful implementation of a new service and the impact that this new service may have on existing services, one of the major factors is the imposition of unrealistic timescales on the project. Shortcutting development and testing due to unfeasible timescales is a sure-fire way to increase risk and thereby reduce the likelihood of successful implementation. The business must talk to the service provider in the early stages of any development to understand the risks associated with tight timescales, either to the detriment of existing services or the new service, and in contravention of existing development safeguards. This ensures informed business-based decision-making and joint discussion of options for risk mitigation.

User Acceptance Testing

User Acceptance Testing (UAT) must be carried out for all new services prior to implementation. This not only allows the end-users (or their representatives) the opportunity to verify that a new service meets their needs, but also provides a further opportunity for the service provider to verify the operability of the new service in a 'real business world' environment, with real users and to verify that the Service Delivery organisation is geared-up to support the new service.

Changes to service requirements

Any variance to the standard (as defined in the SLA) service, either ad-hoc or permanent, must be requested according to a clearly laid-down process and timescales agreed and detailed in the SLA. Business Users must be aware that they have a commitment to respect these timescales and not expect the service provider to be able to satisfy requests for service availability that are not made by the proper agreed channels and to the agreed timescales (although service providers will always do their best).

Control processes

All new services are, when implemented into a 'live' environment, placed under the management of the service providers existing service control processes. It is therefore imperative that these control processes are considered prior to go-live in the context of the new service business requirements and that necessary details are provided to the relevant Service Support and Delivery personnel in good time. Failure to consider this requirement may lead to a potentially unsupported (and insupportable) service with severe consequences to the affected user community.

6.3 Service reporting

A significant amount of data is collated and monitored by IS in the daily delivery of quality service to the business; however, only a small subset is of real interest and importance to the business. The majority of data and its meaning is more suited to the internal management needs of IS.

The business likes to see a historical representation of the past period's 'performance' that portrays their experience; however, it is more concerned with those historical events that continue to be a threat going forward, and how IS intend to militate against such threats.

Cross-referenced data must still be presented which align precisely to any contracted, chargeable elements of the delivery; which may or may not be 'technical' depending upon the business focus and language used within contracts and SLAs.

It is not satisfactory simply to present reports which depict adherence (or otherwise) to SLAs, which in themselves are prone to statistical ambiguity. IS needs to build a solutions-oriented approach and content to reporting; i.e. this is what happened, this is what we did, this is how we will ensure it doesn't impact you again, and this is how we are working to improve the delivery of IS services generally.

A reporting ethos which focuses on the future as strongly as it focuses on the past also provides the means for IS to 'market' its wares directly aligned to the positive or negative experiences of the business.

6.3.1 Reporting policy and rules

An ideal approach to building a Business Perspective service reporting framework is to take the time to define and agree the policy and rules with the business with regards to how reporting will be implemented and managed.

This includes:

- targeted audience(s) and the related business views on what the service delivered is
- agreed definitions of all terms and boundaries
- basis of all calculations
- reporting schedules
- access to reports and medium to be used
- meetings scheduled to review and discuss reports.

6.3.2 The right content for the right audience

Numerous policies and rules can exist as long as it is clear for each report which policies and rules have been applied, e.g. one policy may be applied to manufacturing whereas a variant may be more suited to the sales team. However all policies and rules form part of the single reporting framework.

Once the framework, policies and rules are in place, targeting suitably styled reports becomes simply a task of translating flat historical data into meaningful business views (which can be automated). These need to be annotated around the key questions, threats, mitigations and improvements such data provokes. Reports can then be presented via the medium of choice, e.g. paper-based hard copies, on-line soft copies, web-enabled dynamic HTML, current snapshot whiteboards, or real-time portal/dashboards.

Simple and effective customisable and automated reporting is crucial to a successful, ongoing reporting system that is seen as adding value to the business. Over time, many of the initial standard reports may become obsolete in favour of the regular production of custom reports which have been shaped to meet changing business needs and become the standard.

The end result is the targeted recipient having clear, unambiguous and relevant information in a language and style they understand and like, accessible in the medium of their choice, and detailing the delivery of IS into their environment within their boundaries, without such information being clouded by the data related to the delivery of IS into other areas of the business.

Figure 6.2 depicts the service reporting process.

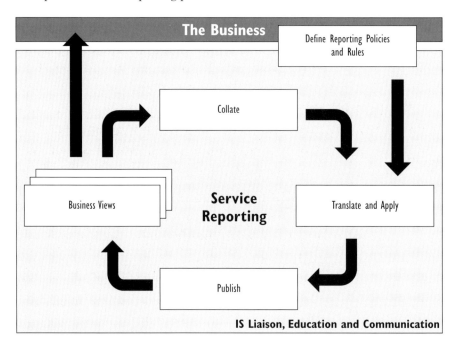

Figure 6.2 – Service reporting process

6.4 Education

Throughout this chapter and the rest of book many references have been made to areas of education which can be deployed across IS to underpin the Business Perspective approach. Education consists of training or awareness collateral that is both delivered and available or scheduled for future provision.

All training should be aligned to the Business Perspective. This core material should be scheduled and delivered across IS, as relevant to each individual's roles and responsibilities, to existing and new staff as they join, with updates to staff provided through the regular communications process. It important to ensure that all training material is kept up to date.

Examples of specific education to underpin the Business Perspective approach are:

- business language and terminology and how IS terminology can and should be translated when liaising with the business

- business strategy, objectives and plans, and how IS aligns to and supports these

- business organisation, key people and how the IS organisation aligns and interfaces

- business culture(s), how this manifests itself in the business/IS touch points, and IS alignment and behaviours

- business processes and where IS underpins these, in terms of roles and activities and the IS contribution, i.e. understanding the value of IS in the business value chain

- how and where each system underpins business processes, especially as in today's complex ICT environments where this is not a one-to-one relationship, but a highly complex multi-dependent relationship

- detailed knowledge of critical business processes and Vital Business Functions (VBF), specifically the business-critical elements and their IS dependence

- SLAs and OLAs to understand the business requirements for service quality, especially in the context of IS roles and responsibilities

- Portfolio of Services and Service Catalogue for an awareness of how IS is positioned and marketed within the business

- Business/IS communication and liaison processes, including service reporting for an awareness of how and what service performance is communicated to the business

- spending time in business to understand and appreciate the pressures they face, the demands and dilemmas

- customer service excellence to facilitate enjoyable customer experiences at all points of interaction

- business change programmes, the objectives, plans and IS's role and contribution, plus impacts for existing services

- process integration across the business and IS, e.g. Change Management

- new/changed services to support business change and business development, especially significant for the Service Desk

- IS process training, especially those processes of high significance to the business, e.g. security and IT Service Continuity

- ISG policies and standards

- Balanced Scorecards for awareness of IS objectives and measurement

- Supplier contracts and SLAs to understand supplier commitments and responsibilities, plus supplier interfaces processes.

7 SUPPLIER RELATIONSHIP MANAGEMENT

Many suppliers provide support services and products which have a relatively minor, and fairly indirect, role in value generation, but a significant few provide services and products which make a direct and important contribution to value generation and the implementation of the overall business strategy.

The greater the contribution the supplier makes to business value, the more that supplier needs to be involved both in contributing to the development of business strategy, and in realising that strategy. The smaller the supplier's value contribution, the more likely it is that the relationship will be managed mainly at an operational level, with limited interaction with the business.

Similarly, the type of service or product that a supplier provides can set the level for the relationship. For example, an organisation's supplier of mainframe application hosting services may need to be closely involved in planning strategic business initiatives (such as entry into a new market, or a competitor take-over), whereas a supplier of a relatively small or specialist service or product may interact purely at an operational level.

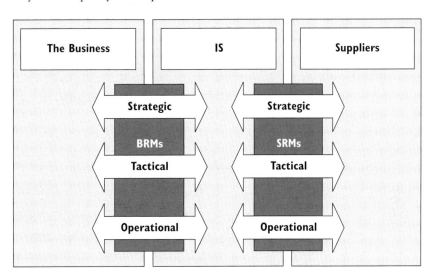

Figure 7.1 – Relationship management (levels of interaction)

The level at which the supplier is managed can be defined as follows:

- **strategic**: for significant 'partnering' relationships which involve senior managers sharing confidential strategic information to facilitate long-term change plans.
- **tactical**: for relationships involving more commercial activity and some business interaction (e.g. business change, risk), as well as 'business as usual' at the operational level.
- **operational**: for suppliers which provide low value and/or readily alternatively sourced products or services.

To help the reader understand the management approach most suitable for each of their supplier relationships, this chapter explores different types of supplier relationship, the way they are formalised, and how they are managed according to their business significance.

Strategically important relationships are given the greatest focus; it is in these cases that Supplier

Relationship Managers (SRMs) have to ensure that the Business Perspective is extended into the supplier domain so that the relationship works beyond the initial contract, and evolves in line with business developments.

The aim of this chapter is to raise awareness of the business context of working with suppliers, and how this work can best be directed toward realising business benefit for the organisation. For the remainder of this chapter, references to 'services' may be taken to mean services and/or products where applicable.

7.1 Types of supplier relationship

The rise in popularity of external sourcing, and the increase in the scope and complexity of some sourcing arrangements, has resulted in a diversification of types of supplier relationship. At a strategic level it is important to understand the options that are available so that the most suitable type of supplier relationship can be established to gain maximum business benefit.

When selecting a supplier a number of factors need to be taken into consideration including track record, capability, references, credit rating and size relative to the business being placed. In addition, depending on the type of supplier relationship, there may be personnel issues which need to be considered.

Whilst it is recognised that factors may exist which influence the decision on type of relationship or choice of supplier (e.g. politics within the organisation, existing relationships), it is essential that in such cases the reasoning is identified and the impact fully assessed to ensure costly mistakes are avoided.

7.1.1 Internal supplier

In many organisations, IS is set up as a supplier to the organisation, identifying the cost of and in some cases, charging for, its services. This approach can be adopted for various reasons:

- **to reduce costs or influence behaviour**: staff typically view IS products and services as free. Making them more aware of the cost of the services that they use can significantly affect their use of resources. This can result in reduced costs for the organisation as a whole

- **as a first step towards outsourcing IS**: part of the process of becoming an internal supplier involves defining the services, roles and responsibilities of IS. Having these clearly identified makes it easier to establish what needs to be covered in any outsourcing contract

- **to improve the quality of service provided**: through competition with external suppliers, IS is required to become more quality-conscious. Additionally, resources become concentrated in the areas where demand existed, something that is visible under the more formal arrangements.

Internal suppliers need to be commercially viable but often with a focus on the interests of the organisation rather than on profitability.

7.1.2 Single, dual or multi-sourced supply

Services may be sourced from a single supplier or multi-sourced. Services are most likely to be sourced from two or more competing suppliers where the requirement is for standard services or products that are readily available 'off the shelf'. Multi-sourcing is most likely to be used where cost is the prime determinant, and requirements for developing variants of the services are low, but may also be undertaken to spread risk. Suppliers on a multi-source list may be designated with 'Preferred Supplier' status within the organisation, limiting or removing scope for use of other suppliers. A single-sourced deal may include clauses on exclusivity and a price advantage may have been negotiated on the basis that the entire organisation uses the supplier's services.

7.1.3 Partnering relationships

Partnering relationships are established at an executive level and are dependent on a willingness to exchange strategic information to align business strategies. Many strategically important customer/supplier relationships are now positioned as partnering relationships. This reflects a move away from traditionally hierarchical relationships, where the supplier acts subordinately to the customer organisation, to one characterised by:

- **strategic alignment**: good communication and information exchange at the strategic level, leading to an alignment of business strategies
- **trust**
- **openness**: when reporting on service performance, costs and risk assessments
- **collective responsibility**: joint partnership teams taking collective responsibility for current performance and future development of the relationship
- **shared risk and reward**: e.g. agreeing how investment costs and resultant efficiency benefits are shared, or how risks and rewards from fluctuations in material costs are shared.

Both parties derive benefits from partnering. An organisation derives progressively more value from a supplier relationship as the supplier's understanding of the organisation as a whole increases, from its ICT inventory architectures through to its corporate culture, values and business objectives. With time, the supplier is able to respond more quickly and more appropriately to the organisation's needs. The supplier benefits from a longer-term commitment from the organisation, providing it with greater financial stability, and enabling it to finance longer-term investments, which benefit its customers.

A partnership makes it possible for the parties to align their ICT infrastructures. Joint architecture and risk control agreements allow the partners to implement a range of compatible solutions from security, networking, data/information interchange, to workflow and application processing systems. This integration can provide service improvements and lowered costs through:

- extranets improving information flow
- integrated service delivery processes
- automated bill payment systems
- integrated data access systems.

Such moves also reduce risks and costs associated with one-off tactical solutions, put in place to bridge a supplier's ICT with that of the organisation.

The key to a successful partnering relationship is being absolutely clear about the benefits and costs such a relationship will deliver before entering into it. Both parties then know what is expected of them at the outset.

7.1.4   Outsourcing

This term is sometimes used more specifically to refer to the transfer of an internal service function to an external service provider, with other terms such as 'externalising' or 'external sourcing' then being used to refer to other direct external sourcing arrangements. An outsourcing arrangement often involves the transfer of assets (capital assets, licences, staff, etc.), with the customer retaining just a core of expertise sufficient to manage the relationship. Where the transfer of staff is included as part of the outsourcing agreement, care needs to be taken to ensure compliance with the appropriate legislation. Not only can the matter become complex from a legal perspective but, to ensure a smooth transition with minimal complications, resource must be made available to provide effective communication to staff and to manage personnel issues.

Outsourcing has been used by organisations for many years for facilities management services (such as catering or cleaning) but it has also become an increasingly popular option for IS. Examples range from maintenance of legacy systems, to development of leading edge systems to hosting new business services, and from discrete application services, to data centres and entire IS units. Service Desks, telecoms, web-related services and the support and/or maintenance of networks and desktops, are other common examples.

An important preparatory step in establishing a successful supplier relationship is the identification of services that are suitable for outsourcing. In addition to the potential benefits listed in Chapter 2, other practical considerations which influence the selection of a service or group of services are:

- **operational**: grouping services into cohesive bundles to reduce the degree of business process interaction within the organisation or with other suppliers

- **outsourcing strategy**: does the organisation's IS unit intend to act as a 'value-add' integrator of services from several suppliers, or is the strategy for wholesale outsourcing?

- **market analysis**: which groups of services can practically be outsourced with reasonable expectations of success? Market analysis assesses the maturity, capability and experience of suppliers against possible service groupings

- **volatility**: services may be selected on the basis that they are least likely to be affected by change (e.g. legacy systems maintenance), and these form relatively stable contracts. However, it may also be appropriate to outsource volatile services, particularly if specialist suppliers have greater scale, capacity and expertise to react to highly volatile business requirements. Although in this scenario, the service provider may include contingency costs because of the increased risk due to volatility

- **aggregation**: the merits of using one organisation to act as 'prime' contractor, managing several other contracts. This allows the business to concentrate on managing a smaller number of strategically significant relationships.

Outsourcing may be undertaken at different levels of significance to the value chain:

- infrastructure: non-core operational functions, and ICT with least significance to the value chain

- business process: business applications and/or Business Process Outsourcing (BPO) with direct contribution to the value chain

- business transformation: Business Transformation Outsourcing (BTO) covers a holistic approach to strategic business development and sourcing policy with direct contribution to value development.

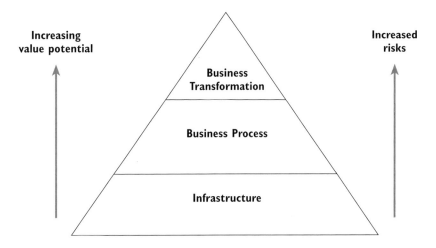

Figure 7.2 – Outsourcing levels

For many organisations the chosen outsourcing 'level' may represent a balance between strategic transformation requirements and risk. The circumstances vary for every organisation. However, in each case the result needs to be demonstrable improved value for the organisation. The *Application Management* book further discusses sourcing strategies.

7.1.5   Consortia

A supply contract may be established with a group of suppliers, typically with one supplier positioned as the 'Lead Supplier', and is expected to appear as a single entity to the organisation. This situation may result when a supplier decides to form co-operative partnerships with other companies which have complementary competencies to maximise their collective chances of securing a contract. The situation may also occur as a tactical stage in a supplier rationalisation programme, where the organisation seeks to reduce the number of its supplier relationships by contract aggregation. A number of smaller supplier contracts may be novated to a strategic supplier.

7.1.6   Joint ventures

Outsourcing may be implemented through a new company, partly owned by one or more organisations, and a supplier – a joint venture. This form of strategic partnership may be underpinned by some transfer of equity between the parties.

Particularly in areas where the pace of technology change is fast, large companies have often found they can achieve market position quicker through alliances with smaller specialist companies, rather than developing services anew. These relationships may involve partial or complete acquisition of the specialist company.

Tip

To select successfully the most appropriate type of supplier relationship, there needs to be a clear understanding of the business objectives that are to be achieved.

7.2   Characterising relationships

A number of factors, from the nature of the service to the overall cost, determine the importance of a supplier from a Business Perspective. As shown later, the greater the business significance of a supplier relationship, the more the business needs to be involved in the management and development of a relationship.

A strategic positioning tool such as that illustrated in Figure 7.3 can help to establish this importance.

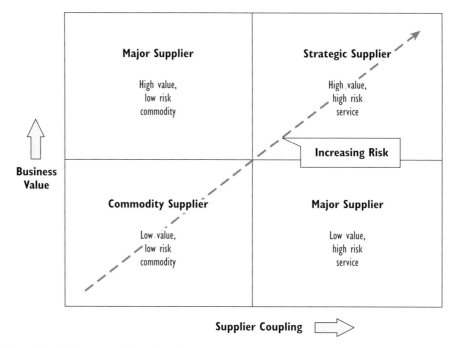

Figure 7.3 – Profiling a supplier relationship

Business Value

The Business Value, measured as the contribution made to the business value chain, provides a more business-aligned assessment than pure contract price.

Supplier coupling

The more standard the services being procured, the lower the dependence the organisation has on the supplier, and the more readily the supplier could be replaced (if necessary). Standardised services support the business through minimal time to market when deploying new or changed business services, and in pursuing cost-reduction strategies.

The more customised those services are, the greater the difficulty in moving to an alternative supplier. Customisation may benefit the business, contributing to competitive advantage through differentiated service, or may be the result of operational evolution.

Tailored services increase the dependence on the supplier, increase risk and can result in increased cost. From a supplier perspective, tailored services may decrease their ability to achieve economies of scale through common operations, resulting in narrowed margins, and reduced capital available for future investment.

Standard products and services are the preferred approach unless a clear business advantage exists, in which case a strategic supplier delivers the tailored service.

> **Tip**
>
> **High-value or high-dependence relationships involve greater risks for the organisation. These relationships need comprehensive contracts and active relationship management.**

7.3 Formalising a supplier relationship

Having established the type of supplier, the relationship then needs to be formalised. In the discussion below the term 'agreement' is used generically to refer to any formalisation of a relationship between customer and supplier organisations, and may range from the informal to comprehensive legally binding contracts. Simple, low-value relationships may be covered by a supplier's standard terms and conditions, and be managed wholly by IS. A relationship of strategic importance to the business, on the other hand, requires a comprehensive contract which ensures that the supplier supports evolving business needs throughout the life of the contract. A contract needs to be managed and developed in conjunction with procurement and legal departments, and business stakeholders.

> **Tip**
>
> **The agreement is the foundation for the relationship. The more suitable and complete the agreement, the more likely it is that the relationship will deliver business benefit to both parties.**

7.3.1 Agreement coverage

The nature and extent of an agreement depends on the relationship type and an assessment of the risks involved.

A pre-agreement risk assessment is a vital stage in establishing any external supplier agreement. For each party it exposes the risks which need to be addressed and needs to be as comprehensive as practical, covering a wide variety of risks including financial, business reputation, operational, regulatory and legal.

A comprehensive agreement minimises the risk of disputes arising from a difference of expectations. A flexible agreement, which adequately caters for its adaptation across the term of the agreement, is maintainable and supports change with a minimum amount of re-negotiation.

The contents of a basic service agreement are:

- **basic terms and conditions**: the term (duration) of the contract, the parties, locations, scope, definitions, and commercial basis
- **service description**: the functionality of the services being provided, along with constraints on the service delivery, such as performance, availability, capacity, technical interface and security. Service functionality may be explicitly defined, or in the case of well-established services, included by reference to other established documents, such as a Service Catalogue
- **service standards**: the service measures, and the minimum levels which constitute acceptable performance, e.g. IS may have a performance requirement to respond to a request for a new desktop system in 24 hours, with acceptable service deemed to have occurred where this performance requirement is met in 95% of cases. Service levels must be realistic, measurable and aligned to the organisation's business priorities.
- **workload ranges**: the volume ranges within which service standards apply, or for which particular pricing regimes apply.
- **Management Information (MI)**: the data which must be reported by the supplier on operational performance – take care to ensure that MI is focused on the most important or headline reporting measures upon which the relationship will be assessed. Key Performance Indicators (KPIs) and Balanced Scorecards (BSCs) may form the core of reported performance data.
- **responsibilities and dependencies**: description of the obligations of the organisation (in supporting the supplier in the service delivery efforts) and of the supplier (in its provision of the service).

An extended service agreement may also contain:

- service debit and credit regime (incentives and penalties)
- performance criteria.

The following gives a limited sample of the legal and commercial topics typically covered by a contractual agreement:

- scope of services to be provided
- service performance requirements
- division of responsibilities
- contract review and dispute resolution processes
- price structure
- payment terms
- commitments to change and investment
- agreement change process

- confidentiality and announcements
- intellectual property rights and copyright
- liability limitations
- termination rights of each party
- obligations at termination and beyond.

7.3.2   Documentation approach

The final form of an agreement, and some of the terminology, may be dictated by the views and preferences of the procurement and legal departments, or by specialist legal firms.

Tip

Seek legal advice when formalising external supply agreements.

Formal contracts

Contracts are appropriate for external supply arrangements which make a significant contribution to the delivery and development of the business.

Contracts provide for binding legal commitments between customer and supplier, and cover the obligations each organisation has to the other from Day 1 of the contract, often extending beyond its termination. A contract is used as the basis for external supplier agreements where an enforceable commitment is required. High-value and/or strategic relationships are underpinned by a formal contract. The formality and binding nature of a contract are not at odds with the culture of a partnering agreement, but rather form the basis upon which trust in the relationship may be founded.

A contract is likely to be structured with a main body containing the commercial and legal clauses, and with the elements of a service agreement, as described earlier, attached as schedules. Contracts may also include a number of other related documents as schedules, for example:

- security requirements
- business continuity requirements
- mandated technical standards
- migration plans (agreed pre-scheduled change).

Most large organisations have procurement and legal departments specialising in sourcing contracts. Specialist legal firms may be employed to support the internal procurement and legal function when establishing significant formal contracts.

The management of contracts within a life cycle is dealt with in Section 7.4.

Service Level Agreements

In ITIL an SLA is defined as a 'written agreement between a service provider and the customer(s) that documents agreed service levels for a service'.

The IS practitioner should be aware that Service Level Agreements are widely used to formalise service-based relationships, internally and externally, and that whilst conforming to the definition above, these agreements vary considerably in the detail covered.

The views of some organisations, such as the Chartered Institute of Purchase and Supply (CIPS) and various specialist lawyers, are that SLAs ought not to be used to manage external relationships unless they form part of an underlying contract. *The Complete Guide to Preparing and Implementing Service Level Agreements* (2001) emphasises that stand-alone SLAs may not be legally enforceable but instead 'represents the goodwill and faith of the parties signing it'. Therefore it is in customers' and suppliers' interests to ensure that SLAs are incorporated into an appropriate contractual framework, which meets the ITIL objective that SLAs are binding agreements.

SLAs should be reviewed on a regular basis to ensure performance conforms to the service levels that have been agreed.

Operational Level Agreements

The organisation is likely to be dependent on its own internal support groups to some extent. To be able to achieve SLA targets, it is advisable to have formal arrangements in place with these groups. Operational Level Agreements (OLAs) ensure that underpinning services support the business/IS SLA targets. OLAs focus on the operational requirements that the services need to meet. This is a non-contractual, service-oriented document describing services and service standards, with responsibilities and obligations where appropriate.

Just as with SLAs, it is important that OLAs are monitored to highlight potential problems. The Service Level Manager has the overall responsibility to review performance against targets so that action can be taken to remedy, and prevent future recurrence of, any OLA breaches. Depending on the size of the organisation and variety of services, e.g. SLAs and OLAs, a Service Delivery Manager should take responsibility for their service or set of services. See Chapter 8 for more details on the Service Delivery Manager's role.

Supplier Catalogue

The Supplier Catalogue is a list of the organisation's suppliers, together with details of the products and services that they provide to the business (e.g. email service, PC supply and installation, Service Desk). The Supplier Catalogue contains supplier details, a summary of each product/service (including support arrangements), information on the ordering process and, where applicable, contract details. Appendix B.2 provides an example of the sort of data that a Supplier Catalogue holds.

Supplier Catalogues are beneficial because they can be used to promote preferred suppliers and to prevent purchasing of unapproved or incompatible items. By co-ordinating and controlling the buying activity, the organisation is more likely to be able to negotiate preferential rates.

Adding to, removing from, or amending items in the Supplier Catalogue needs to be handled via the Change Management process, to ensure that any impact is assessed and understood.

In most organisations the Supplier Catalogue is owned by the procurement department, which acts as an interface between the business and the supplier.

7.4 Contract Management

7.4.1 The contract life cycle

When dealing with external suppliers, it is recommended that a formal contract is established. Figure 7.4 outlines the stages of the contract life cycle.

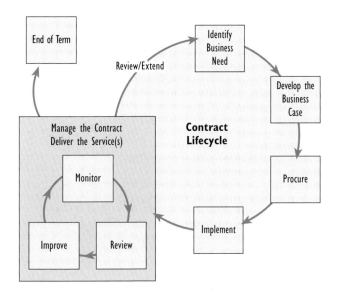

Figure 7.4 – The contract life cycle

Identify business need:

- Statement of Requirement (SOR)
- initial business case
- conformance to strategy/policy.

Develop the Business Case:

- options (internal, external)
- costs
- timescales
- benefits
- initial risk assessment.

Procure:

- identify method of procurement
- establish evaluation criteria
- evaluate
- select
- award.

Implement:

- set up the service
- transition of service.

Manage the contract/deliver the service(s):

- delivery of service/products
- monitor (service and costs), review, improve
- manage (risks, changes, failures, improvements, relationship)
- review against business need
- plan for closure/renewal/extension.

End of term:

- review (determine benefits delivered, ongoing requirement).

The contract life cycle requires input from three key areas within the organisation:

Business:

- identifying the initial and ongoing business need
- developing the SOR
- selecting the solution
- ensuring conformance of the solution with the overall business direction.

IS unit:

- providing technical advice on the options that are available to meet the need
- selecting the solution
- managing integration and ongoing technical performance of the chosen solution.

Procurement:

- selecting the solution
- leading the procurement of the chosen solution
- legal terms and conditions
- providing advice during the life of the contract
- value for money.

All three areas need to be jointly involved with selecting the solution and with managing the ongoing performance of the supplier. Each area takes responsibility for the interests of their own area, whilst being aware of the implications to the other areas.

7.4.2 Reviews

Formal reviews need to take place throughout the contract life cycle to minimise risk and ensure the business realises maximum benefit from the contract. Reviews are built in to each stage of the life cycle but the focus of the reviews changes as the life cycle progresses. Initial reviews concentrate on making the key decisions regarding the scope and structure of the contract; later reviews look at the resourcing and progress of the project or service; whereas reviews held after implementation focus on ensuring the contract is performing as required. The latter of these is covered in more detail in Section 7.4.3. The key benefits of holding reviews throughout the contract life cycle are to ensure:

- the project or service is correctly resourced in terms of experience/skills
- the ongoing feasibility is assessed on a regular basis, thus giving a greater chance of success

- communication on the status of the project or service
- cost and timescales are monitored and more likely to be achieved.

A final review is held to identify the overall result of the contract and to capture lessons learnt. This information is used as input into future contracts.

7.4.3 Contract reviews

Contract reviews must be undertaken on a regular basis to ensure the contract is continuing to meet business needs. Contract reviews assess the contract operation holistically and at a more senior level than the service reviews that are undertaken at an operational level. They consider:

- how well the contract is working
- its relevance for the future
- whether changes are needed
- what the future prognosis for the relationship is.

Topics to be covered in a review include:

- information exchange on business strategy and direction, potential future requirements
- supplier input on market direction, new developments which may benefit the business
- commercial performance of the contract, reviews against benchmarks or market assessments, suitability of the pricing structure and charging arrangements
- review of escalated disputes
- authorisation of updates to contract documentation
- review of major change proposals and/or initiatives
- provision of guidance on future contract direction, and ensuring best practice management processes are established.

Dependent on the scale and nature of the contract, the contract review or dedicated meetings may be held in respect of:

- contract change proposals
- direction and governance of strategy.

Contract reviews need to be linked to SLM reviews, considering escalated issues, and communicating policies and priorities.

7.4.4 Contract Change Management

Where a supplier relationship has been entered to provide competitive advantage to the business (through a differentiation strategy), this advantage is only maintained where new innovations and improvements are continually explored and implemented ahead of the organisation's competitors. There needs to be close and well-maintained alignment between the business's product and services development strategy, and related dependencies on new or changed supplier services.

For high-value, lengthy or complex supply arrangements, the period of contract negotiation and agreement can be lengthy, costly, and may involve a protracted period of negotiation. It can be a natural inclination to wish to avoid further changes to a contract for as long as possible. However for the business to derive full value from the supplier relationship, the contract must be able to be regularly and quickly amended to allow the business to benefit from service developments.

Contract changes are expedited where:

- the obligations of both parties are clearly established in the contract
- the roles and responsibilities are defined for the respective operational, technical, commercial, legal and executive stakeholders
- different types and scale of change are recognised, impacted and approved only by appropriate stakeholders.

Changes will vary in extent from minor operational changes (which may need no contract change at all) through to major strategic change initiatives requiring major renegotiation.

7.5 Managing the relationship

For the relationship to be successful, a number of key areas need to be managed:

- supplier performance
- benefits
- financial performance
- risk
- change
- business perception and satisfaction.

These management efforts are controlled through the relationship's governance arrangements.

7.5.1 Governance arrangements

The governance body is drawn from appropriate stakeholders at different levels within each organisation, and is structured so that the organisation's representatives face-off to their counterparts in the supplier's organisation. Defining the responsibilities for each representative, meeting forums and processes ensure that each person is involved at the right time, in influencing or directing the right activities.

The exact structures depend on factors such as:

- the scale and importance of the relationship
- the nature of the services
- each organisation's internal structure.

Governance structures need to establish:

- who should be involved in the relationship and why
- who meets whom, how often and to what end
- a balanced relationship across the organisations
- escalation routes
- dispute resolution processes
- communications processes.

The scale and importance of the relationship influences the governance arrangements. The more significant the relationship, the greater the involvement with the business and procurement department. Figure 7.5 extends Figure 7.1 to show how the extent and seniority of the interaction reduces with less significant suppliers.

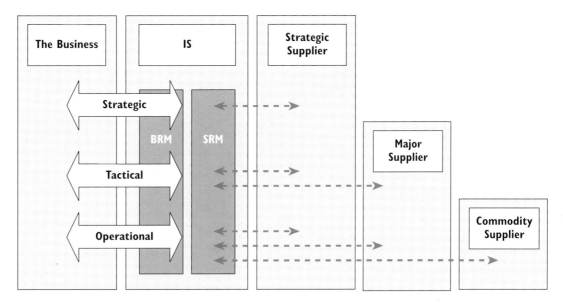

Figure 7.5 – Different governance models

A governance structure for a strategic relationship needs representation on at least the following levels:

- **strategic/executive interests**: for any deal it is important that in each organisation a single point of ultimate responsibility is clearly established. This person must be:
  - a peer with their opposite number
  - empowered to make financial decisions and to resolve any disputes arising in relation to the contract
  - responsible for the success of the contract within their organisation
  - able to represent all views on behalf of other stakeholders in their organisation.

- **tactical interests**: contracts management covering commercial, legal and business development interests.

- **operational/IS service delivery interests**: the IS unit is the operational home for the relationship, where the SRM is responsible for the effectiveness of the day-to-day operation of the relationship and delivery of services. The SRM needs to ensure that they are as aware as possible of policies and agreements reached at senior meetings, and communicate regularly on the relationship performance to the contract manager and the responsible executive.

IS needs to liaise regularly with the organisation's procurement department to ensure that the commercial objectives of the relationship are being fulfilled.

7.5.2 Supplier Relationship Manager (SRM) and Business Relationship Manager (BRM) liaison

A key objective for the SRM is to ensure that the value of a supplier to the organisation is fully realised. Value is realised through all aspects of the relationship, from operational performance assurance, responsiveness to change requests and demand fluctuations, through to contribution of knowledge and experience to the organisation's strategic change processes. In large organisations there may be several SRMs, each having responsibility for one or more of the organisation's major supplier relationships. In such organisations regular communication needs to take place between SRMs to identify areas where centralised management of suppliers could bring additional benefits to the organisation.

Example

A large multi-national company had software agreements in place with the same supplier in no less than 24 countries. By arranging a single global licensing deal with the supplier, the company made annual savings of US$11,000,000.

A BRM ensures that suitable contacts are established within a Business Unit to allow IS to interact at the different levels (operational to strategic), and for all the Service Management disciplines. A large IS unit may need to have different BRMs for different Business Units. Therefore, there can be a complex interaction between multiple SRMs and BRMs; with a BRM needing to co-ordinate requirements on behalf of a Business Unit with multiple SRMs, and an SRM having to liaise with multiple BRMs to ensure that their supplier gains a comprehensive view of the business.

Large organisations with major supplier relationships may also require different people to be involved at the different levels of engagement. An SRM may be responsible for contract ownership and review, and authorising tactical change, but may facilitate strategic change through senior or executive engagements. At the operational level, the SRM is likely to be supported by IS, who work with their opposite numbers in the supplier's organisation, to ensure the ongoing effectiveness of service delivery processes. When several people are involved, care must be taken to ensure that the way the supplier relationship is managed by the organisation is delivering maximum benefit.

Example

A nationwide retail organisation had an overall SRM owning the management of their major Network Services supplier. However, services, contracts and billing were managed by several individuals spread throughout the organisation. The SRM put forward a business case for single ownership of the supplier and all the various contracts, together with consolidation of all the individual invoices into a single quarterly bill. The estimated cost savings to the organisation were in excess of £600,000 per annum.

BRMs may have similar levels of structure, depending on the level of engagement needed with the Business Unit. Between them, the interaction of the SRMs and BRMs is vital to ensure that the suppliers' perspective is aligned with the Business Perspective.

7.5.3 Supplier performance management

The IS unit, through Service Level Management (SLM), must ensure that the supplier's priorities match the business's priorities. The supplier must understand which of its service levels are most significant to the business, and the IS unit must be instrumental in managing that connection through the SLM processes. Major efficiencies benefiting both organisations can be realised through the integration of the supplier's and the organisation's processes. This is facilitated the more both organisations are ITIL conformant in all disciplines.

Formal, documented service review meetings must be held on a regular basis to review the supplier's performance against service levels, at a detailed operational level. These meetings provide an opportunity to check that the ongoing service performance management remains focused on supporting business needs. Typical topics include:

- service performance against SLA
- incident and problem reviews
- business and customer feedback
- escalated issues, and contract review summaries
- demand management
- expected major changes which will (or may) affect service during the next service period
- key business events over the next service period which need particular attention from the supplier (e.g. quarter end processing)
- Service Improvement Programmes (SIPs)
- benchmarks
- best practice assurance and standards compliance (e.g. BS 15000, ISO 9000).

The SRM provides agreed summaries of performance to contract review meetings.

Major service improvement initiatives are controlled through SIPs. Progress of existing SIPs, or the need for a new initiative, is reviewed at service review meetings.

Service Improvement Programme

Procedures need to be agreed for dealing with any failures on the part of the supplier. Generally this is through the introduction of a SIP.

Forward-thinking organisations not only use SIPs to deal with failures but also to improve a consistently achieved service. It is important that a contract provides suitable incentives to both parties to invest in service improvement.

Customer satisfaction surveys

Tools such as customer satisfaction surveys also play an important role in revealing how well supplier service levels are aligned to business needs. A survey may reveal instances where there are dissatisfied customers, yet the supplier is apparently performing well against its contract (and vice versa). This may happen where service levels are inappropriately defined and should result in a review of the contract.

7.5.4   Benefits management

The benefits management process must ensure that:

- benefits are defined and understood up front

- IS and business benefits are linked and complementary
- benefits are measured and managed to ensure they are delivered
- the benefits case is updated in the light of change.

It must be possible for the organisation to answer the question – 'Is this relationship working for me?'

For those significant supplier relationships in which the business has a direct interest, both the business (in conjunction with the procurement department) and IS will have established their objectives for the relationship, and defined the benefits they expect to realise. This forms a major part of the business case for entering into the relationship.

These benefits must be linked and complementary, and must be measured and managed. Where the business is seeking improvements in customer service, then IS supplier relationships contributing to those customer services must be able to demonstrate improved service in their own domain, and how much this has contributed to improved customer service.

For benefits assessments to remain valid during the life of the contract, changes in circumstances that have occurred since the original benefits case was prepared must be taken into account. A supplier may have been selected on its ability to deliver a 5% saving of annual operational cost compared with other options, but after two years has delivered no savings. However, where this is due to changes to contract, or general industry costs which would have also affected the other options, it is likely that a relative cost saving is still being realised. A maintained benefits case shows that saving.

Benefits assessments often receive lower priority than cost-saving initiatives, and are given less priority in performance reports than issues and problem summaries, but it is important to the long-term relationship that achievements are recognised. A benefits report must make objective assessments against the original objectives, but may also include morale-boosting anecdotal evidence of achievements and added value.

Tip

It is important for both organisations, and for the longevity of the relationship, that the benefits being derived from the relationship are regularly reviewed and reported.

7.5.5 Financial performance

An assessment of the success of a supplier relationship, from a Business Perspective, is likely to be substantially based on financial performance. Even where a service is performing well, it may not be meeting one or both parties' financial targets. It is important that both parties continue to benefit financially from the relationship. A contract which squeezes the margins of a supplier too tightly may lead to under-investment by the supplier, resulting in a gradual degradation of service, or even threaten the viability of supplier. In either case this may result in adverse business impacts to the organisation.

The business has expectations for the financial performance over the term of a contract. Budgets are established against this expectation, and the business case for entering the contract is dependent on it. The business may be expecting stable or reducing service charges where some rationalisation or economy of scale is expected (e.g. through consolidation of Service Desks, deployment of a common desktop, or consolidation of intranets).

The business may have budgeted for increasing charges, particularly where it has been agreed that the supplier will make a capital investment which would otherwise need to have been made by the organisation (e.g. replacement of an internal aged data centre with an outsourced or managed service). The supplier has expectations on margin and total revenue.

At the time of contract signing, negotiations should have established cost models and a charging structure which meets these expectations, achieving financial equilibrium.

Both organisations are able to realise these expectations unless this equilibrium is disturbed by:

- costs of service delivery being higher than expected
- additional unexpected unrecoverable charges exceeding budget (e.g. consultancy services)
- either party seeking to improve its position at the expense of the other.

The total costs of service delivery may increase due to many factors, including:

- an overly intrusive approach by the organisation into the supplier's operation, increasing the supplier's workload through responses to queries and perhaps even implementation of changes which may impact the supplier's ability to deliver economies of scale
- the organisation failing to meet its obligations to the supplier, either in the way it uses services (e.g. users failing to use the correct channels for reporting incidents to a Service Desk) or in failing to provide resources required by the supplier to be able to deliver its services (e.g. a data centre connection).

Where the organisation's business has a justified increased service demand or requirements for additional scope, the equilibrium is maintained as long as the additional charges are proportionate to the parameters of the original agreement, i.e. a fair price.

The key to the successful long-term Financial Management of the contract is a joint effort directed towards maintaining the financial equilibrium, rather than a confrontational relationship delivering short-term benefits to only one party.

Cost must be constantly in focus for SIPs and change initiatives. Working together, the relationship management teams may identify improvements in:

- the supplier's service delivery operation
- the operational interface between the organisation and the supplier: minor changes to scope, presentation, or user education may significantly improve overall efficiency (e.g. where users understand how to contact the Service Desk and the information they are required to provide, they save themselves and the Service Desk analysts significant amounts of time)
- the consumption of the supplier's services: reduction in unnecessarily high consumption of services reduces the organisation's costs (e.g. long-term retention of e-mail messages, especially ones with large attachments, significantly increases the storage requirements for an e-mail service, even perhaps requiring investment in additional storage capacity)
- sources of cost overrun: high number of incidents, exceptions to process, quality

defects in inputs, poor performance of any of the organisation's Information Systems or networks upon which the supplier is dependent.

Financial Management tools

In long-term relationships it is useful to ensure that there are controls or mechanisms in the contract to commit a supplier to improvements in service and/or cost so that the business maintains or improves its position against its competitors. These controls also help to ensure that the financial expectations of both parties are met. Controls include:

- benchmarks against the market
- Activity Based Costing (ABC) of the supplier's operation
- audits
- cost-reduction initiatives undertaken in conjunction with SIPs
- incentives and penalties (service debits and service credits).

Audits and/or ABC analysis can help to improve confidence and trust through openness, especially when charges for additional or changed services are being negotiated.

Tools such as benchmarking provide an assessment against the marketplace. The supplier may be committed by the contract to maintaining charges against a market rate. To maintain the same margin, the supplier is obliged to improve its operational efficiency in line with its competitors. Collectively these tools help provide an assessment of an improving or deteriorating efficiency.

The use of service credits (penalties) and service debits (incentives) in contracts can be effective in ensuring that the supplier's priorities are directed toward those issues with the greatest business impact. To be effective from a Business Perspective, service credit and debit schemes need to:

- provide disincentives against cutting costs, which then result in an SLA breach
- be prioritised, with the highest penalties being allocated to the SLA breaches with the greatest impact on the business, and provide rewards where the business receives most benefit through over-performance/achievement, thus incentivising improved delivery
- be simple enough to administer, whilst meeting their objectives
- be regularly reviewed and updated to ensure they remain aligned to business impact
- not be sufficiently punitive as to threaten the viability of the supplier.

Service credit schemes should never be regarded as a revenue source for an IS organisation. If the service credit is so onerous that it imposes excessive financial penalties upon the supplier, the result may be that the supplier is unable to invest in service improvement. The objective should be an improvement in the service, not punishment of the supplier.

Paying the bills

Delays or disputes in paying the supplier's invoices ultimately benefit neither party. The organisation needs to ensure that adequate controls are in place to validate invoices, but that processes and systems ensure timely payment. The contract may permit the supplier to make additional charges in respect of late payment.

Analysis of invoice-related incidents by finance managers, supported by IS managers as needed, help to maintain a good working relationship. Invoices may need to be supported by detailed breakdown information to allow cross-charging back to multiple Business Units. Financial

Management for IT services as described in the *Service Delivery* book provides a comprehensive model for use when reviewing and agreeing supplier invoices.

7.5.6   Risk Management

Risk Management from the Business Perspective, in the context of working with suppliers, centres on assessing vulnerabilities in supplier arrangements which pose threats to any aspect of the business including:

- customer satisfaction
- brand image
- market share
- share price
- profitability
- regulatory impacts or penalties (in some industries).

The nature of the relationship affects the degree of risk to the business.

Risks associated with an outsourced supplier are likely to be greater in number, and more complex to manage, than with an internal supply. It is rarely possible to 'outsource' risk. Blaming a supplier does not impress customers or internal users affected by a security incident or a lengthy system failure. New risks arising from the relationship need to be identified and managed, with communication and escalation as appropriate.

A substantial risk assessment should have been undertaken pre-contract, but this needs to be maintained in the light of changing business needs, changes to the contract scope, or changes in the operational environment.

Risk profiles and responsibilities

The organisation and the supplier must consider the threats posed by the relationship to their own assets, and have their own risk profile. Each must identify their respective risk owners. In a well-functioning relationship it is possible for much or all of the assessment to be openly shared with the other party. By involving supplier experts in risk assessments, especially in Operational Risk Assessments (ORAs), the organisation may gain valuable insights into how best to mitigate risks, as well as improving the coverage of the assessment. Appendix B.4 provides guidance on ORAs.

Business Impact Analysis

When evaluating risks of disruption to business services or functions, the business may have different priorities for service/function restoration. It may be that for a limited period of time a reduced customer service is acceptable, with concentration focused on core products/services. During an extended disruption, staff payroll functions may be given a high priority, whilst staff development and training initiatives are postponed indefinitely.

Business Impact Analysis (BIA) is the tool used to assess the impacts on different areas of the business, resulting from a loss of service. Appendix B.5 illustrates a BIA template. The BIA considers how the impact changes, the longer the service loss continues. This impact analysis is used, in conjunction with cost assessments of potential countermeasures, in the Risk

Management processes to establish which countermeasures should be implemented, and in Business Continuity Management (see below) to determine the recovery time requirements for different services.

The BIA also informs Availability Management and IT Service Continuity Management processes, and therefore involves the SRM in the development of the BIA to ensure supplier aspects are considered and included where appropriate.

Business Continuity Management

Business Continuity Management (BCM) covers all aspects of ensuring that the business continues to operate, following a major incident or disaster. This includes:

- provision of alternative premises and related services
- provision of alternative equipment, including ICT
- staff relocation
- contingency plans and processes
- crisis management roles and responsibilities.

IT Service Continuity Management (ITSCM) is one element in this overall BCM effort, and needs to integrate with the other elements (see the *Service Delivery* book for more information on ITSCM and the *PAS 56 Guide to Business Continuity Management* for guidance on BCM best practice). Where the continuity requirement is only for a reduced business service during a disaster, then the IT Service Continuity Plan may only need to cater for 50% or less of normal network and server capacity, number of desktops, etc.

The extent of the continuity solution required is a balance between the potential impact on the business (given in the BIA), and costs of contingency measures. Typically it is most cost-effective for contingency arrangements to be made through a specialist continuity services provider.

Different sorts of contingency arrangements for services provided by the supplier might be made, for example:

- by the supplier using their own alternative resources
- by the supplier subcontracting to a continuity services provider
- by the organisation using an alternative supplier.

In practice, IS needs to liaise between the business and the supplier to identify the best balance between increased contingency costs and the reduction in business risk. This requirements process, the responsibilities for sourcing the continuity arrangements, the responsibilities for producing a Business Continuity Plan and the respective crisis management responsibilities all need to be established as part of the original supplier contract. This ensures that all responsibilities are understood and bound by contract.

Long-term agreement risks

Earlier in the chapter a number of benefits which could be gained from a long-term supply agreement were discussed; however, there are also some new risks which need to be managed.

Lock-in

There is a danger that, over time, services may become progressively customised for the organisation, making it harder to seek alternative more favourably priced sourcing in the future. Many 'standard' IS product sets can be readily extended and customised. The maintenance of such implementations, and the implications on lock-in to the supplier, must be considered. The supplier may be attracted towards customisation where this:

- provides additional revenue
- increases the supplier lock-in
- improves the supplier's image as being responsive.

IS has a role to play in promoting standardisation with its suppliers, and in appraising the business to limit customisation to clear value-generating activities.

Erosion of competitive position

The business position against its competitors may be compromised where it has long-term supplier contracts which do not keep track with best-in-market prices, especially where the price trend is downward. The competitive position may also be compromised where total charges increase beyond expectation with time, possibly as a result of customisation. Contracts with best-in-market price commitments – supported by benchmarking, demand management, and contract change processes which ensure that changes have a business case – are all tools which help to mitigate these risks.

Erosion of service performance

The business can be impacted in many ways if the performance of key suppliers degrades over time. Service performance is likely to degrade over time where a supplier fails to make adequate investment in its infrastructure. A supplier responsible for managing network file servers may be inclined to maximise its margins by delaying upgrades as long as possible. This is particularly likely to happen towards the end of a contract period where renewal is unlikely. It must be ensured in advance that the contract/SLA defines performance, capacity and availability service levels, and that performance against these levels is supported by an incentive/penalty scheme which rewards proactive systems management.

7.5.7   Supply chain management

A business service may be dependent on a number of internal and/or external suppliers for its delivery. These may include a mixture of service providers and commodity suppliers. Some suppliers supply directly to the organisation, others are indirect, i.e. via another supplier. Direct suppliers are managed by the organisation's SRM; indirect suppliers are managed by the relevant supplier. Any one supplier may provide products or services used to support a number of different business services.

Supply chain analysis shows the mapping between business services and supplier services. Analysis of business processes will reveal the suppliers involved in each process, and the points of hand-off between them.

Management of the supply chain ensures that functional boundaries and performance requirements are clearly established for each supplier to ensure that overall business service levels are achieved. Business services are most likely to meet their SLAs consistently where there are a small number of suppliers in the supply chain, and where the interfaces between the suppliers in the chain are limited and simple.

Reducing the number of direct suppliers reduces the number of relationships which need to be managed, the number of peer-to-peer supplier issues which need to be resolved, and reduces the complexity of the SRM's task. Some organisations may successfully collapse the whole supply chain around a single service provider, often referred to as a 'prime' supplier. Facilities management is often outsourced to a single specialist service provider, who may in turn subcontract restaurant services, vending machine maintenance and cleaning.

Outsourcing entire business services to a single 'prime' may run additional risks:

- business: creation of a competitor (vertical integration)
- operational: outsourcing elements of service outside the prime's core competence may reduce service effectiveness, whilst also incurring additional cost.

For these reasons organisations need to carefully consider their supply chain strategies ahead of major outsourcing activity. The scope of outsourced services needs to be considered to reduce the number of suppliers, whilst ensuring that it fits typical competencies in the supply market.

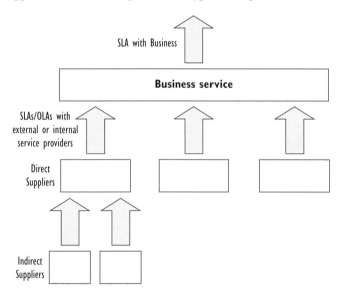

Figure 7.6 – Supply chain mapping

Ensuring quality throughout the supply chain

For any organisation it is important to ensure quality throughout the complete supply chain. There are various methods, concepts and standards that can be employed to help to achieve this, including:

- **ITIL**: use of ITIL can help to ensure processes are integrated across the business and IS, focusing on the alignment of IS with business requirements, including quality of service
- **BS 15000**: specifies an integrated set of interrelated management processes to deliver managed services effectively to the business and its customers. BS 15000 is aligned with, and complementary to, ITIL
- **ISO 9000**: is the international standard for quality in business
- **ESCM**: The eSourcing Capability Model for service providers enables IT-enabled service providers to evaluate and improve their capability to provide consistently high-quality outsourcing services in the Internet economy.

When using suppliers, the business does not have direct control over the quality of the products and services that are provided. However, choosing suppliers that implement and conform to the same standards and industry best practices as the organisation, not only helps to ensure the quality of their products and services, but also leads to better communication between the parties through common terminology and understanding.

7.6 Developing the supplier relationship

7.6.1 Building a relationship

Building relationships takes time and effort. As a result, the organisation may only be able to build long-term relationships with a few key suppliers.

The experience, culture and commitment of those involved in running a supplier relationship are at least as important as having a good contract and governance regime. The right people with the right attitudes in the relationship team can make a poor contract work, but a good contract does not ensure that a poor relationship team delivers.

A considerable amount of time and money is normally invested in negotiating major supplier deals, with more again at risk for both parties if the relationship is not successful. Both organisations must ensure that they invest suitably in the human resources allocated to managing the relationship.

The personality, behaviours and culture of the relationship representatives all influence the relationship. For a partnering relationship, all those involved need to be able to respect and work closely, and productively, with their opposite numbers.

Recognition needs to be made and addressed at the outset of possible human tensions. If IS has become responsible for the day-to-day operation of a supplier contract borne through outsourcing, then, for instance, people may be suspicious, resentful and adversarial in their dealings. A concern that success of the relationship may lead to further outsourcing of their or their colleagues' jobs, is certainly not the basis for a dynamic, proactive, partnering type approach!

Formal relationship planning may, in the service provider's case, be based on an account plan defining further business opportunities, and in the customer's case through a relationship development plan. It is important that these objectives are shared and compatible if a genuine partnering approach is sought.

7.6.2 Building on trust

As trust increases between the parties, both may gain business benefit. Business strategy may be shared earlier and more extensively, improving efforts to align service developments to future business need. At the operational level, improved trust may lead to more efficient IS integration, closer operational inter-working leading to a lowering of service delivery cost. Trust results from experience and is only established over time in a relationship which is successful for both parties. Trust can be lost considerably more quickly than it is established!

7.6.3 Building on knowledge

By understanding the organisation's needs and tailoring the service to meet those needs, the supplier can increase customer loyalty and potentially improve its market share. As the supplier's knowledge of the organisation's business improves, the more effective the supplier becomes in helping the business to exploit technology opportunities for business advantage.

7.6.4 Ending a relationship

The point of responsibility within the organisation for deciding to change a supplier relationship is likely to depend on the type of relationship. IS may have identified a need to change supplier, based on the existing supplier's performance, but for a contractual relationship the decision needs to be taken in conjunction with the organisation's procurement and legal departments.

The organisation should take careful steps to:

- perform a thorough impact assessment of a change of supplier on the organisation and its business, especially during a period of transition. This could be particularly involved in the case of a strategic relationship

- make a commercial assessment of the exit costs. This may include contractual termination costs if supplier liability is not clear, but the largest costs are likely to be associated with a transition project. For any significant-sized relationship this typically includes a period of dual-supply as services are migrated. Any IS change associated with a change in supplier will increase costs, either immediately as fixed costs, or over time where borne by the supplier and reflected back in service tariffs

- take legal advice on termination terms, applicable notice period and mechanisms, and any other consequences, particularly if the contract is to be terminated early.

- reassess the market to identify potential benefits in changing supplier.

A prudent organisation undertakes most of these steps at the time the original contract is established, but needs to refresh that assessment when a change of supplier is being considered.

7.7 Day-to-day working with suppliers

At an operational level, integrated processes need to be in place between an organisation and its suppliers to ensure efficient day-to-day working practices, for example:

- Is the supplier expected to conform to the organisation's Change Management process?

- How does the Service Desk notify the supplier of incidents?

- How is CMDB information updated when CIs change as a result of supplier actions?

These and many other areas need to be addressed to ensure smooth and effective working at an operational level. To do so, all touch points need to be identified and procedures put in place so that everyone understands their roles and responsibilities. However, an organisation should take care not to automatically impose its own processes but to take the opportunity to learn from its suppliers.

Example

A contract had been let for a bespoke Stores Control System for which the
organisation's IS department had developed processes to support the live system
once it was installed. This included procedures for recording and documenting
work done on the system by field engineers (e.g. changes, repairs, enhancement
and reconfigurations). At a project progress meeting the supplier confirmed that
they had looked at the procedures and could follow them if required. However,
having been in this situation many times before, they had already developed a set
of procedures to deal with such events. These procedures were considerably more
elegant, effective and easier to follow than those developed by the organisation.

In addition to process interfaces, it is also essential to identify how issues are handled at an
operational level. By having clearly defined and communicated escalation routes, issues are likely
to be identified and resolved earlier, minimising the impact. Both the organisation and the
supplier benefit from the early capture and resolution of issues.

Both sides should strive to establish good communication links. The supplier learns more about
the organisation's business, its requirements and its plans, helping the supplier to understand and
meet the organisation's needs. In turn, the organisation benefits from a more responsive supplier
who is aware of the business drivers and any issues, and is therefore more able to provide
appropriate solutions.

Close day-to-day links can help each party to be aware of the other's culture and ways of working,
resulting in fewer misunderstandings and leading to a more successful and long-lasting
relationship.

7.8   Challenges when working with suppliers

There are a number of challenges that may arise when working with suppliers:

- working with a non-ideal contract
- managing significant change in parallel with delivering existing service
- legacy issues, especially with services recently outsourced
- insufficient expertise retained within the organisation
- being tied in to a contract which has punitive penalty charges for early exit
- situations where the supplier depends on the organisation in fulfilling the service
  delivery (e.g. for a data feed) can lead to issues over accountability for poor service
  performance
- service delivery failures, especially those associated with culpability disputes
- disputes over charges
- interference by either party in the running of the other's operation
- being caught in a daily fire-fighting mode, losing the proactive approach
- communication, not interacting often enough, or quick enough or focusing on the
  right issues

- personality conflicts
- one party 'milking' the relationship, resulting in win-lose changes rather than joint win-win changes
- losing the strategic perspective, a 'cannot see the wood for the trees' issue and losing touch with the relationship objectives.

Key elements that can help to avoid these issues are:

- a well-defined, well-managed contract
- a mutually beneficial relationship
- clearly defined (and communicated) roles and responsibilities on both sides
- good interfaces and communications between the parties
- well-defined Service Management processes on both sides.

8 ROLES, RESPONSIBILITIES AND INTERFACES

If IS is truly to adopt the Business Perspective approach to service provision it is essential that the roles and responsibilities of everyone concerned are clearly defined and agreed and that the scope and ownership of each of the processes are also agreed and documented. These roles and responsibilities should therefore be adapted to fit the individual requirements of each organisation according to its size, nature, structure, culture and geographical distribution. In small organisations one or two people within IS perform all of the roles, whereas in large organisations there may be teams of people working in each area.

Normally the key process areas related to the Business Perspective approach are located within the IS unit of an organisation. However, in some organisations the function is located within the business. The location of the function is irrelevant – what is crucial is the role. The role, wherever it is located, should have the same fundamental objectives of business/IS alignment and the exploitation of IS services, to maximise business benefit. The remainder of this section outlines specific roles and responsibilities applicable to the function, whether it is located within the business, within IS, or some combination of the two. The actual roles used in this section are not important. Some organisations may choose to combine or split specific roles. However, it is important that all of the responsibilities are assigned and that there are no gaps between the agreed responsibilities.

Wherever the Business Perspective related roles are located, their scope and objectives should be set by the business within which they operate. Often this area within IS is referred to as a Business Relationship or Customer Relationship unit. Together these roles provide a business focus to all other IS and Service Management processes and personnel. The following sections give indications as to the main responsibilities of the various roles involved within such a unit.

8.1 The overall IS role and the interactions

The overall IS management function accountable for the progression of the Business Perspective approach has a responsibility to:

- be an active member of the IS Steering Group (ISG)
- create an environment within which all of the supporting processes can achieve their objectives and satisfy the needs of the business, customers and users
- play a key role within the business change programme and in crisis management
- ensure that all areas of IS are marketed within all areas of the business to ensure that business use and benefit derived from IS services are maximised
- co-ordinate, manage and control all aspects of the Business Perspective approach, including the definition and scope of all of the supporting processes and the interfaces to all other business and IS processes
- maintain and wherever possible improve the quality of service provided by IS, instigating appropriate remedial actions, in conjunction with SLM and the SIP
- provide a focal point for the co-ordination and management of all issues relating to the business, customers and users, and also all supplier-related issues

- ensure that plans and strategies for the development of the Business Perspective approach are produced and circulated regularly to senior business and IS managers

- ensure that any projects and changes to IS services are appropriately assessed and the impact and risks are made clear to manage the expectation of the business, customers and users

- ensure that there are appropriate plans for the recruitment and training of all staff working on the Business Perspective approach

- ensure that long-term and effective relationships with suppliers and partners are developed that underpin the requirements of the business, customers and users

- ensure that regular reviews of all the key process areas are performed.

The scope and interaction between some of the major roles are illustrated in Figure 2.4.

8.2   The IS Steering Group role

To ensure that business and IS strategies and plans remain synchronised, many organisations form a joint co-ordinating body called an IS or ICT Steering Group (ISG). This body consists of senior management representatives from various business areas and IS. The function of the ISG is to meet regularly and review both the business and IS plans and strategies to ensure that they are aligned as closely as possible across all Business Units and at all levels, as illustrated in Figure 4.7.

The ISG ensures that unrealistic timescales are not imposed or attempted by either the business or IS, which could jeopardise quality or disrupt normal operational requirements. The business and IS work together within the ISG, on the plans and strategies for IS, to ensure that the priorities and timescales of IS objectives, projects and changes are continually adjusted to reflect the changing needs of the business and that corresponding changes within budgets are made to reflect these adjustments.

8.3   The Communications Manager role

The Communications Manager or Marketing Manager has a key responsibility for the development of effective and efficient communication processes. Further responsibilities of the role are to:

- liaise with all business, customer and user groups, ensuring that all areas of the business are aware of IS capabilities and are also aware of their own responsibilities in relation to the IS services provided

- develop, produce and implement the IS communications plan

- co-ordinate and control all communications between IS and the business

- maintain relationships with communications managers and contact points within the business

- continually raise the awareness of the business within IS

- assist all areas of IS to market their services to the business

- ensure that all IS business and marketing plans are produced and maintained.

8.4   The Business Relationship Manager role

The prime responsibility of a Business Relationship Manager (BRM) is to develop efficient and effective relationships with the business. The responsibilities of the BRM role are to:

- manage the perception and expectation of the business, customers and users

- ensure that the correct processes are in place so that Business Relationship Management achieves its objectives and that they are subjected to continuous improvement

- understand current and planned new business processes and their requirements for services

- regularly take the customer journey and sample the customer experience, providing feedback on customer issues to IS (this applies to both IS customers and also the external business customers in their use of IS services)

- conduct and complete customer surveys, assist with the analysis of the completed surveys and ensure that actions are taken on the results

- act as an IS representative on user groups

- provide a single contact and escalation point for all IS issues

- develop a full understanding of business, customer and user strategies, plans, business needs and objectives

- maintain the IS Portfolio of Services and proactively market and exploit its use within all areas of the business

- work with the business, customers and users to ensure that IS provide the most appropriate levels of service to meet business needs currently and in the future

- ensure that IS are working in partnership with the business, customers and users, developing long-term relationships

- promote service awareness and understanding

- raise the awareness of the business benefits to be gained from the exploitation of new technology

- facilitate the development and negotiation of appropriate, achievable and realistic SLRs and SLAs between the business and IS

- facilitate the negotiation of fair and equitable service charges with business, customers and users

- be flexible and responsive to the needs of the business, customers and users

- provide liaison on all project matters and support the Change and Release Management processes in the protection of the operational environment

- participate and contribute to the management and direction of IS

- assist with the introduction, development and maintenance of Business Continuity Plans and IT Service Continuity Plans

- ensure the business, customers and users understand their responsibilities/commitments to IS (i.e. IS dependencies)

- assist with the maintenance of a register of all outstanding improvements and enhancements.

8.5 The Supplier Relationship Manager role

The prime responsibility of a Supplier Relationship Manager (SRM) is to develop efficient and effective relationships with the suppliers, outsourcers and partners. The responsibilities of the SRM role are to:

- manage all suppliers to ensure that they continue to meet or exceed their contractual targets both currently and in the future

- manage supplier and contractual risk and measure all aspects of supplier performance, instigating remedial actions whenever and wherever necessary

- conduct service and contractual reviews with all major suppliers on a regular basis

- manage all aspects and stages of the contract life cycle

- maintain a catalogue of suppliers, services, products and contracts

- measure the perception of the business, customers and users

- ensure that the correct processes are in place so that Supplier Relationship Management achieves its objectives and that they are subjected to continuous improvement

- provide a single liaison and contact point for all supplier and contractual issues

- develop a full understanding of supplier strategies, plans, business needs and objectives

- work with suppliers to ensure that IS provide the most appropriate levels of service to meet business needs currently and in the future

- ensure that IS are working in partnership with suppliers developing long-term relationships

- facilitate the development and negotiation of appropriate, achievable and realistic contracts and contractual targets with suppliers

- facilitate the negotiation of 'value for money' services and products with all suppliers

- ensure wherever possible that suppliers use ITIL best practice and that their processes support and interface with all IS processes, especially Change Management.

8.6 The Service Delivery Manager role

The Service Delivery Manager's role normally revolves around the operation and delivery of a service or set of services. Therefore they may have to deal with many different business and customer contacts dealing with any issues that may arise within their area of responsibility. The sets of services should be aligned wherever possible with Business Units so that business managers talk with a small number of Service Delivery Managers. In some organisations this role may have the title of Service Delivery Improvement Manager, Service Manager or even Service Improvement Manager; however, throughout the rest of this section the term Service Delivery Manager is used.

In some ways, the Service Delivery Manager's role is similar to that of the BRM in that both bridge the gap between the business and IS. However, the emphasis of the role is different. The BRM focuses on strategic issues, working with the business in support of future needs through the use and exploitation of IS capability, whilst the Service Delivery Manager focuses on the day-to-day operational issues associated with the delivery of current and planned services, ensuring that they meet business requirements. The Service Delivery Manager is also responsible for co-ordination with other Service Delivery Managers where the complexity of services delivered to a single Business Unit is such that multiple Service Delivery Managers are required to manage the day-to-day operational issues.

The major additional responsibility of the Service Delivery Manager over and above that of the BRM is that of co-ordination of their role with the role of all other Service Delivery Managers, especially those Service Delivery Managers who may deal with the same customer groups.

The responsibilities of the Service Delivery Manager role are to:

- manage the expectation of the Business Units, customers and users concerning the use of the particular service(s)

- measure the perception of service quality from the business's, customer's and user's perspective, and regularly produce reports that are subsequently reviewed with the relevant customers

- ensure that the correct processes are in place so that the Service Delivery Managers achieve their objectives and that the processes and services are subjected to continuous improvement activities

- provide a single point of contact, liaison and escalation for all service-related matters and to support the Change and Release Management processes in the protection of the operational environment

- regularly take the customer journey and sample the customer experience, providing customer feedback to IS

- understand the business processes supported by IS services and the criticality of those processes

- conduct and complete customer surveys, assist with the analysis of completed surveys and ensure that actions are taken on the results

- develop an understanding of business, customer and user strategies, plans, business needs and objectives related to the particular service(s) and ensure that SLR and SLA targets are matched to those needs

- work with all service contacts to ensure that IS provide the most appropriate levels of service to meet business needs currently and in the future

- facilitate the negotiation of fair and equitable service charges with the business, customers and users

- be flexible and responsive to the needs of the business, customers and users

- assist with the introduction, development and maintenance of service availability, security and recovery plans

- promote service(s) awareness and understanding and co-ordinate all the activities of all other areas and processes within IS related to the appropriate service(s), especially SLM, BRMs and SRMs

- ensure the business, customers and users understand their service responsibilities/commitments to IS

- assist SLM to ensure that existing services meet their service targets and that planned new services meet their timescales and the targets are realistic and achieved

- develop and maintain a register of all outstanding service improvements and enhancements.

8.7   The Account Manager role

The role of the Account Manager is very similar to aspects of the Business Relationship Manager (BRM) and the Service Delivery Manager, but also emphasises the marketing and selling of all aspects of IS to the business, customers and users, particularly in the development of new opportunities and the winning of new customers. Account Managers work closely with the Communications Manager and their objectives are to maximise each Business Unit's use of IS and to maximise the use of all IS services. Therefore their additional responsibilities over and above those of Service Delivery Managers and BRMs are to:

- find and win business opportunities and new customers

- proactively use the Service Catalogue, the Portfolio of Services and information relating to all of the existing live services, development services and proposed new services to market IS to all areas of the business, thus exploiting the use of IS services within the business for maximum business benefit.

- ensure that subsequent investment in IS services and ICT infrastructure is targeted at those areas that yield the greatest opportunity and return.

9 SUMMARY

This *Business Perspective* book focuses on the areas illustrated in Figure 2.2:

- **People**: the people involved within IS in the provision of services to the business
- **Processes**: the IS processes involved in the effective delivery of quality services to the business
- **Technology**: the technology, products and tools used to deliver the services to the users and customers of IS, either internal or external
- **Suppliers**: the suppliers, vendors and partners used to assist with the support and delivery of IS services.

These four aspects have been covered within the various chapters of this book, with Chapter 8 focusing on the roles and responsibilities of those involved within the Business Perspective associated processes. In this last section the emphasis is on the processes. The objective of the Business Perspective processes is to provide a top-down, business-aligned approach to IS. This flows from the strategically oriented planning and business relationship processes, through all areas of IS and its suppliers, using the liaison and supplier relationship processes. Figure 9.1 illustrates the four Business Perspective process areas and their major deliverables.

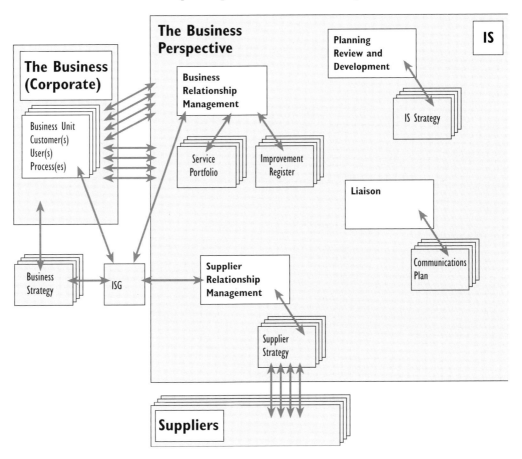

Figure 9.1 – The Business Perspective processes

The scope and goal of each of these four processes is described in detail in the following sections.

9.1 Planning, review and development process

This process, together with the business relationship process, provides the information, relationship and long-term direction from the business, that enable IS to be aligned with a Business Perspective. When considered from a Business Perspective and using best practice, strategy and planning are driven by the business into all its lines of business and its Business Units using its governance framework, as outlined in Chapter 4.

The formality of such frameworks varies from organisation to organisation. Where business best practice is adopted, business plans and strategies are developed taking into account the strategy of the business and IS value chain functions. Business strategy is influenced primarily by market and customer opportunities along with associated strategies for products and business services sold into those markets. From an IS perspective, IS can influence the markets, customers, products and business services where the IS value chain functions of services and technologies can influence the business's primary market-facing strategies.

Business strategy is also influenced in a secondary manner by opportunities in the value chain functions, which can improve their internal performance by organising or making better use of their capabilities.

The planning, review and development process activities enable IS to be closely aligned with the business's current, and future, requirements and processes. It drives the business/IS governance framework top-down, from strategy and planning through development and delivery to support and operations, covering all ITIL process areas, as illustrated in Figure 9.2.

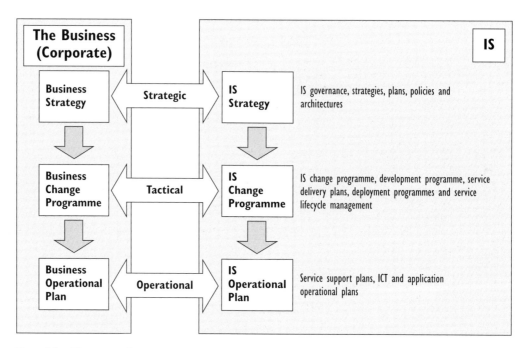

Figure 9.2 – Alignment – from strategy to operations

The goal of the planning, review and development process is:

> **'To develop and maintain business alignment with all IS services and processes both currently and in the future.'**

The scope of the process includes activities for:

- working with ISG and the business in the development and maintenance of IS governance, strategy, policies, plans and prioritisation
- ongoing alignment of the business and IS strategies, policies, plans and priorities
- ongoing alignment of the business and IS change programmes
- ongoing alignment of the business and IS operational plans
- developing relationships with business strategists and planners and interfaces to strategic business planning processes
- assisting BRMs in developing and maintaining the Portfolio of Services
- working with ISG and BRMs in the ongoing maintenance of the IS change programme
- providing advice and guidance on IS governance
- agreeing and documenting all IS strategic processes ensuring effective interfaces with the business and its strategic processes
- ensuring that all IT Service Management processes use ITIL best practice, end-to-end processes, fully integrated and wherever possible that are owned, controlled and directed by business processes and process owners
- facilitating and stimulating business and IS innovation
- improving IS ability to deliver service and its capability and agility to adapt to meet changing business and technology needs
- working with IS Finance and running IS as a business within a business
- ensuring that all improvement activities are incorporated into an overall SIP
- documenting all planning processes.

The detailed content of these activities is explained in greater in detail in Chapters 4 and 5.

9.2 Business Relationship Management process

The objective of this process is to understand the nature of the relationship between the business and IS and to encourage the business to take the lead in a working partnership with IS. As mentioned earlier relationships need to be developed at strategic, tactical and operational levels between IS and the business.

The goal of the business relationship management process is:

> **'To develop and maintain effective and efficient relationships with all Business Units at all levels.'**

The scope of the process includes activities for:

- establishing and improving working relationships with all areas of the business
- Portfolio Management and developing and maintaining the Portfolio of Services
- aligning and continuing to align IS service to the needs of the business and its individual Business Units
- understanding the role of IS within the business value chain and ensuring that the services and processes support their operation effectively and efficiently

- ensuring that IS strategies, policies and plans reflect the current and future needs of their individual Business Units and their managers

- facilitating and stimulating business and IS innovation

- developing relationships with stakeholders, Informed Customers, key customers and other key business contacts

- managing and tracking all customer interactions and transactions with IS

- documenting all business relationship processes.

The detailed content of these activities is explained in greater detail in Chapters 4 and 5.

9.3 Liaison, education and communication process

This process area focuses on IS staff and provides mechanisms enabling IS staff to undertake their work adopting a Business Perspective, irrespective of how remote their activities are from the day-to-day operation of the business. It also examines the processes needed to make IS staff business-aware and to help them in all liaisons and contacts they may have with the business. It provides process advice on how and what IS should communicate with the business and deals with improving internal relationships and awareness of IS staff so that they are business and IS aware and are not limited to their own professional IS 'silos'.

Processes for liaison, education and communication must be well managed and adequately funded to create the balanced technical and process-focused staff that IS and the business need.

The goal of the liaison, education and communication process is:

'To maintain high levels of business awareness and focus throughout IS using effective communication.'

The scope of the process includes activities for:

- developing and maintaining relationships with all areas of IS

- developing and maintaining the IS communications plan

- improving the culture and the business focus throughout all areas of IS

- providing all areas of IS with information on business processes and requirements

- improving business information flows and providing business documentation and information to all areas of IS

- understanding the business view, business processes, products and services, ensuring that all areas of IS understand the role of IS within the business value chain and their responsibilities within them

- providing a single information base on all aspects of the business

- measuring, collecting, correlating, analysing and reporting of all customer and business metrics for all of the Business Perspective related processes, together with all of the other customer- and business-related metrics, providing consolidated customer feedback to all areas of IS

- liaising and co-ordinating between planning, Business Relationship Management and Supplier Relationship Management processes and activities and all other ITIL processes and IS personnel

- developing and providing training seminars and workshops
- documenting all liaison processes.

The detailed content of these activities is explained in greater in detail in Chapters 3, 4 and 6.

9.4 Supplier Relationship Management process

Supplier management process and relationships are dealt with by focusing on the relationships required in dealing with all types of suppliers, vendors and partners, ranging from commodity suppliers through to strategic outsourcing and co-sourcing partnerships. The objective is to act in the same way as other business functions act in outsourcing parts of their service capability and to retain the right services and the right business relationships. This requires the appropriate use of outsourced service providers where they add value, reduce costs or improve the management effectiveness of IS.

The goal of the Supplier Relationship Management process is:

> **'To develop and maintain effective and efficient relationships with all suppliers and partners at all levels.'**

The scope of the process includes activities for:

- establishing and improving relationships with all suppliers and partners
- developing and maintaining an overall supplier strategy, in conjunction with the planning process
- developing and maintaining individual supplier plans and strategies
- developing and maintaining the supplier catalogue
- managing suppliers and contracts consistently, ensuring that all relationships and contracts are effectively managed to deliver value for money, throughout all stages of the contract life cycle
- ensuring that all suppliers products, services and capabilities underpin and align with business value chains, strategies and requirements
- integrating of suppliers' products, processes, services and products with IS processes and services and ultimately business processes, products and services
- ensuring suppliers use ITIL best practice wherever possible and that their strategies and cultures are aligned with the organisation's strategies and cultures
- developing, maintaining and applying supplier evaluation and selection processes
- defining, measuring, analysing, reporting and reviewing standard supplier and contract metrics and measurements
- documenting all supplier processes.

The detailed content of these activities is explained in greater in detail in Chapter 7.

9.5 Conclusion

These four processes should be adopted and adapted on a scale appropriate to the size and complexity of the organisation, and the services and infrastructure to be managed. Whilst it is not essential that all aspects of these processes are implemented, it is essential that all aspects are considered and evaluated with reference to the organisation and its requirements. Different elements of the processes may be used and adapted in different ways to suit the requirements of specific organisations.

Throughout this *Business Perspective* book numerous methods, concepts and techniques have been described. These were introduced principally in Chapters 1 and 2 and further developed and expanded in the subsequent chapters. However, the Business Perspective approach also introduces processes and procedures aimed at developing changes in the culture and mind-sets of people involved in the delivery of IS services. This book emphasises the importance of ongoing alignment of IS cultures, plans and strategies with their business counterparts. It stresses the end-to-end process integration issues and all aspects of communications, especially the education of staff, enabling them to perform their role more effectively in the knowledge that IS objectives are directly mapped to the success of the business as a whole. For too long IS has been seen as separate to the business or at most on the periphery delivering technology to the business. The Business Perspective eradicates that myth, recognising that IS is an integral and vital element of the business as a whole, with processes which map directly into the wider business processes.

10 BIBLIOGRAPHY

Note: entries in this Bibliography are given throughout in alphabetical order of title.

10.1 References

TSO publications

Application Management
OGC
Available from TSO, www.tso.co.uk
ISBN 0-11-330866-3

ICT Infrastructure Management
OGC
Available from TSO, www.tso.co.uk
ISBN 0-11-33865-5

Planning to Implement Service Management
OGC
Available from TSO, www.tso.co.uk
ISBN 0-11-33877-9

Security Management
OGC
Available from TSO, www.tso.co.uk
ISBN 0-11-330014-X

Service Delivery
OGC
Available from TSO, www.tso.co.uk
ISBN 0-11-330017-4

Service Support
OGC
Available from TSO, www.tso.co.uk
ISBN 0-11-330015-8

Other publications

The Balanced Scorecard: Translating Strategy into Action
Robert S. Kaplan, David P. Norton 1996
Harvard Business School Press, Boston
ISBN 0-87584-651-3

Competitive Advantage: Creating and Sustaining Superior Performance
Michael E. Porter 1998
Simon & Schuster
ISBN 0-68-484146-0

The Complete Guide to Preparing and Implementing Service Level Agreements (2nd ed.)
Sheila Pantry and Peter Griffiths 2001
Available from Library Association Publishing
ISBN 1-85604-4106

How to Manage Business Change
OGC
Available from Format Publishing, www.formatpublishing.co.uk and TSO, www.tso.co.uk
ISBN 1-90-309110-1

How to Manage Business & IT Strategies
OGC
Available from Format Publishing, www.formatpublishing.co.uk and TSO, www.tso.co.uk
ISBN 1-90-309102-0

How to Manage Performance
OGC
Available from Format Publishing, www.formatpublishing.co.uk and TSO, www.tso.co.uk
ISBN 1-90-309113-6

How to Manage Service Acquisition
OGC
Available from Format Publishing, www.formatpublishing.co.uk and TSO, www.tso.co.uk
ISBN 1-90-309111-X

How to Manage Service Provision
OGC
Available from Format Publishing, www.formatpublishing.co.uk and TSO, www.tso.co.uk
ISBN 1-90-309112-8

PAS 56:2003 Guide to Business Continuity Management
British Standards Institution/Business Continuity Institute
Available from TSO, www.tso.co.uk
ISBN 0-580-41370-5

Quality Management for IT Services
OGC
Available from TSO, www.tso.co.uk
ISBN 0-11-330555-9

BS 15000: 2003 *Part 2, Simplified Representation of the Relationships*

BS 15000-1:2002 *British Standard for Service Management*

BS 15000-2:2003 *Code of Practice for Service Management*

PD 0005 *IT Service Management – A Manager's Guide*

Recommended websites

www.balancedscorecard.com

www.dti.gov.uk/quality

www.ogc.gov.uk/sdtoolkit/reference/externalsources/naomanagrisk.pdf

www.ogc.gov.uk/sdtoolkit/workbooks/risk/index.html

APPENDIX A LIST OF ACRONYMS AND GLOSSARY

A.1 Acronyms

BCM	Business Continuity Management
BIA	Business Impact Analysis
BRM	Business Relationship Manager
BSC	Balanced Scorecard
BSi	British Standards Institution
CMDB	Configuration Management Database
CMM	Capability Maturity Model
CSF	Critical Success Factor
CSIP	Continuous Service Improvement Programme
EFQM	European Foundation for Quality Management
IC	Informed Customer
ICT	Information and Communications Technology
ICTSG	ICT Steering Group
IS	Information Systems
ISG	IS Steering Group
ISO	International Standards Organisation
IT	Information Technology
ITIL	Information Technology Infrastructure Library
ITSM	Information Technology Service Management
*it*SMF	IT Service Management Forum
ITSCM	IT Service Continuity Management
KPI	Key Performance Indicator
OAT	Operational Acceptance Testing
OGC	Office of Government Commerce
OLA	Operational Level Agreement
ORA	Operational Risk Assessment
RFC	Request For Change

ROI	Return on Investment
SIP	Service Improvement Programme
SLA	Service Level Agreement
SLM	Service Level Management
SLR	Service Level Requirement
SOR	Statement of Requirements
SRM	Supplier Relationship Manager
TCO	Total Cost of Ownership
TQM	Total Quality Management
UAT	User Acceptance Testing
VBF	Vital Business Functions

A.2 Glossary

Balanced Scorecard (BSC)

An aid to organisational Performance Management. It helps to focus, not only on the financial targets but also on the internal processes, customers, and learning and growth issues.

Benchmarking

Benchmarking allows an organisation to compare its performance to that of different organisations or between different units within an organisation.

Business

An overall corporate entity or organisation formed of a number of Business Units to provide a set of products or services, of which IS is one.

Business Continuity Management (BCM)

Anticipating incidents which may affect critical business functions and processes and ensuring that the organisation is capable of responding to such incidents in a planned and rehearsed manner.

Business Customer

A recipient of a product or a service from the organisation itself. For example if the organisation is a bank then this term is used for anyone receiving banking products or services.

Business Impact Analysis (BIA)

Understanding the effect that absence or degradation of a service will have on the business operation.

Business Perspective

An approach which ensures that all IS activities are closely aligned with the business activities and is underpinned by a set of processes focused on achieving that alignment.

Business Relationship Management

> Actively managing the relationships between the business and IS at strategic, tactical and operational levels.

Business recovery plans

> Documents describing the roles, responsibilities and actions necessary to resume business processes following a disruption.

Business Unit

> A segment of the business entity by which both revenues are received and expenditure is caused or controlled, such revenues and expenditure being used to evaluate segmental performance. Usually IS is a separate Business Unit within the overall organisation.

Change Advisory Board (CAB)

> A group responsible for considering requests for change, in terms of technical, business, financial and any other relevant viewpoint. Not necessarily a fixed group of people, but may be different for different kinds of change request.

Change

> An alteration to service or element of the infrastructure that is controlled under Configuration Management, i.e. a change to a Configuration Item (CI).

Change Management

> Process of controlling changes to the infrastructure or any aspect of services, in a controlled manner, enabling approved changes with minimum disruption.

Charging

> The process of establishing charges in respect of Business Units, and raising the relevant invoices for recovery from customers.

Configuration Management

> The process of identifying and defining the Configuration Items in a system, recording and reporting the status of Configuration Items and Requests for Change, and verifying the completeness and correctness of Configuration Items.

Configuration Management Database (CMDB)

> A database that contains all relevant details of each CI and details of the important relationships between CIs.

Contingency Planning

> Planning to address unwanted occurrences that may happen at a later time. Traditionally, the term has been used to refer to planning for the recovery of ICT systems rather than entire business processes.

Continuous Service Improvement Programme

> An ongoing formal programme undertaken within an organisation to identify and introduce measurable improvements within a specified work area or work process.

Contract

> Legally binding agreement between two parties.

Cost

> The amount of expenditure (actual or notional) incurred on, or attributable to, a specific activity or Business Unit.

Costing

The process of identifying the costs of the business and of breaking them down and relating them to the various activities of the organisation.

Critical Success Factor (CSF)

An aspect of delivery which is crucial to success and about which key performance criteria can be set.

Customer

Recipient of the service; usually the customer management has responsibility for the cost of the service, either directly through charging or indirectly in terms of demonstrable business need.

Direct Cost (see also Indirect Cost)

A cost that is incurred for, and can be traced in full to, a product, service, cost centre or department.

End-user

See 'User'.

ICT

Information and Communications Technology – the convergence of Information Technology, Telecommunications and Data Networking Technologies.

Incident

Any event which is not part of the standard operation of a service and which causes, or may cause, an interruption to, or a reduction in, the quality of that service.

Indirect Cost (see also Direct Cost)

A cost incurred in the course of making a product providing a service or running a cost centre or department, but which cannot be traced directly and in full to the product, service or department, because it has been incurred for a number of cost centres or cost units. These costs are apportioned to cost centres/cost units. Indirect costs are also referred to as overheads.

Information Systems (IS)

The overall IS unit/department/organisation responsible for all aspects of the delivery and provision of IS services and the support and management of the ICT infrastructure, including business applications.

Informed Customer (IC)

A member of the business community with the knowledge to enable successful planning, specification, acquisition, implantation and use of IS services that deliver business objectives with agreed resource constraints.

Insourcing

Delivering services using an organisation's own resources.

ISO 9001

The internationally accepted set of standards concerning Quality Management systems.

IS accounting

The set of processes that enable the IS organisation to account fully for the way money is spent (particularly the ability to identify costs by customer, by service and by activity).

IS directorate

That part of an organisation charged with developing and delivering the IS services.

IS service

A described set of facilities, IS and non-IS, supported by the IS service provider that fulfils one or more needs of the customer and that is perceived by the customer as a coherent whole.

IS service provider

The role of IS service provider is performed by any organisational units, whether internal or external, that deliver and support IS services to a customer.

IS Steering Group (ISG)

A joint co-ordinating body to ensure that business and IS strategies and plans remain synchronised.

ITIL

The OGC IT Infrastructure Library – a set of guides on the management and provision of operational IS services.

Key Performance Indicator (KPI)

A measurable quantity against which specific performance criteria can be set.

Known Error

An incident or problem for which the root cause is known and for which a temporary work-around or a permanent alternative has been identified. If a business case exists, an RFC will be raised, but, in any event, it remains a Known Error unless it is permanently fixed by a change.

Operational Level Agreement (OLA)

An internal agreement covering the delivery of services which supports the IS organisation in their delivery of services.

Operational Risk Assessment (ORA)

A risk assessment which focuses on threats which might impact the confidentiality, integrity or availability of operational processes and systems.

Organisational Culture

The whole of the ideas, corporate values, beliefs, practices, expectations about behaviour and daily customs that are shared by the employees in an organisation.

Outsourcing

The process by which functions performed by the organisation are contracted out for operation, on the organisation's behalf, by third parties.

Performance Criteria

The expected levels of achievement, which are set within an SLA or contract, against specific Key Performance Indicators.

Portfolio of Services

A published description of the services that are or will be available and are supported by one or more service providers.

Portfolio Management

The effective management of the IS portfolio through:

- maximising the use of existing IS services within the business

- maximising the investment and return in new and modified IS services

- the identification and retirement of non-profitable services that have outlived their life.

Within the IS services, this process can also be applied to applications and programs.

Problem

Unknown underlying cause of one or more incidents.

Process

A connected series of actions, activities, changes, etc., performed by agents with the intent of satisfying a purpose or achieving a goal.

Provider

The organisation concerned with the provision of IS services.

Quality of service

An agreed or contracted level of service between a service customer and a service provider.

Release

A collection of new and/or changed CIs, which are tested and introduced into the live environment together.

Request for Change (RFC)

Form, or screen, used to record details of a request for a change to any CI within an infrastructure or to procedures and items associated with the infrastructure.

Resolution

Action that resolves an incident. This may be a work-around.

Return on Investment (ROI)

The ratio of the cost of implementing a project, product or service and the savings as a result of completing the activity in terms of either internal savings, increased external revenue or a combination of the two.

Risk

A measure of the exposure to which an organisation may be subjected. This is a combination of the likelihood of a business disruption occurring and the possible loss that may result from such business disruption.

Risk Analysis

The identification and assessment of the level (measure) of the risks calculated from the assessed values of assets and the assessed levels of threats to, and vulnerabilities of, those assets.

Risk Management

The understanding of the risks facing a business process, balanced against the benefits (e.g. of change) and the activities required to set the risks at the level considered appropriate by the business.

Risk reduction measure

Measures taken to reduce the likelihood or consequences of a business disruption occurring (as opposed to planning to recover after a disruption).

Role

A set of responsibilities, activities and authorisations.

Service

One or more IT systems that enable a business purpose.

Service achievement

The actual service levels delivered by the IS organisation to a customer within a defined life-span.

Service Catalogue

Written statement of IS services, default levels and options.

Service Culture

A commitment to delivering the services that the customer requires.

Service Desk

The single point of contact within the IS organisation for users of IS services.

Service Improvement Programme (SIP)

A formal project undertaken within an organisation to identify and introduce measurable improvements within a specified work area or work process.

Service Level

The expression of an aspect of a service in definitive and quantifiable terms.

Service Level Agreement (SLA)

Written agreement between a service provider and the customer(s) that documents agreed service levels for a service.

Service Level Management (SLM)

The process of defining, agreeing, documenting and managing the levels of customer IS service that are required and cost-justified.

Service Level Requirement (SLR)

The service levels required to deliver the service to the customer in a way that delivers the business requirement. It includes an understanding of the resources – hardware, software, financial, human, etc. – that will be required.

Service Management

Management of services to meet the customer's requirements.

Service provider

The unit responsible for the provision of services or products to customers. It can be either internal to the organisation (e.g. IS department) or external (third party or outsource organisation).

Service quality plan

The written plan and specification of internal targets designed to guarantee the agreed service levels.

Stakeholder

Any individual or group that has an interest in the organisation, its activities and its achievements. Examples are customers, partners, employees, shareholders, owners, government and regulators.

Supplier

A third party responsible for supplying underpinning elements of the IS services – suppliers may range from commodity hardware or software vendors, through network service providers and major hardware and software manufacturers to major outsourcing organisations and strategic partnering relationships.

Supplier Relationship Management

Actively managing the relationship between suppliers and IS at strategic, tactical and operational levels.

System

An integrated composite that consists of one or more of the processes, hardware, software, facilities and people, that provides a capability to satisfy a stated need or objective.

Third-party supplier

An enterprise or group, external to the customer's enterprise, which provides services and/or products to that customer's enterprise.

Threat

An indication of an unwanted incident that could impinge on the system in some way. Threats may be deliberate (e.g. wilful damage) or accidental (e.g. operator error).

Total Cost of Ownership (TCO)

All the financial consequences of owning an asset, including depreciation, maintenance, staff costs, accommodation and planned renewal.

Underpinning contract

A contract with an external supplier covering delivery of services that support the IS organisation in their delivery of services.

Urgency

A measure of the time available before the effect of an incident, problem or change is felt by, or increases for, the business process using the service affected.

User

The person who uses the service on a day-to-day basis.

Vulnerability

A weakness of the system and its assets, which could be exploited by threats.

Waterline

The lowest level of detail about the construction or nature of a service that is relevant to the customer.

Work-around

Method of avoiding an incident or problem, either from a temporary fix or from a technique that means the customer is not reliant on a particular aspect of the service that is known to have a problem.

APPENDIX B SAMPLE/TEMPLATE DOCUMENTS

B.1 Balanced Scorecard

Table B.1 – Example Balanced Scorecard design (Source: Balanced Scorecard Functional Standards, Balanced Scorecard Collaborative, Inc.)

Perspective	Cause and Effect Linkage	Objectives	Measures	Targets	Initiatives
Financial	Profitability / Revenue Growth	• Profitable Business Growth	• Operating Income • Sales vs. Last Year	• 20% Increase • 12% Increase	• Likes Program
Customer	Product Quality → Shopping Experience	• Quality Product from a Knowledgeable Associate	• Return Rate • Customer Loyalty – Ever Active % – # units	• Reduce by 50% each year • 60% • 2.4 units	• Quality management program • Customer loyalty program
Internal Process	"A" Class Factories ← Line Plan management	• Improve factory quality	• % of Merchandise from "A" factories • Items in-Stock vs. Plan	• 70% by year 3 • 85%	• Corporate Factory Development Program
Learning and Growth	Factory Relationship Skills / Merchandise Buying/Planning Skills	• Train and equip the workforce	• % of Strategic Skills Available	• Year 1 50% • Year 3 75% • Year 5 90%	• Strategic Skills Plan • Merchants Desktop

B.2 Supplier Catalogue

This Appendix provides an example of the data that a Supplier Catalogue holds. However, it is not exhaustive and each organisation needs to identify the details that they require to help manage their own suppliers. This information should be held in the CMDB for ease of reference and to avoid data duplication.

Supplier name

Contact details (address, telephone, fax, email, website)

Key points of contact (may include):

■ Business Relationship Manager

■ Supplier Service Desk

■ Day-to-day interfaces

■ Escalation point.

Status (to identify preferred suppliers)

Contract information

Contract number

Contract dates (commenced, expiry, review)

Contract details (brief description/summary with a link to the contract itself)

Costs and payment terms

Renewal options

Termination options (particularly how much notice is required)

'Terminate'/'Do Not Renew' indicator and comment. (This is useful, particularly where a large number of suppliers are being managed, to show that a contract is to be terminated/not to be renewed.)

Links to the appropriate CIs (services/products) that have been supplied and/or are being maintained/supported by this supplier.

B.3 Service Catalogue and Portfolio of Services

The Service Catalogue can exist in a variety of forms – often depending on the requirements of the anticipated users of that particular version of the catalogue.

For the IS supplier the major information category to be recorded may be which customers use which service – and the sample Service Catalogue in the *Service Delivery* book reflects this need.

However, with the Business Perspective in mind, it is more likely that we wish customers and users to be made aware of the available services, and what each of those services provides, or could provide, in terms of helping them deliver their business services.

At its simplest the Service Catalogue might be presented to the business as a Portfolio of Services: a list of the available services and for each service a brief description of what they offer to the business, as outlined in Table B.2.

Table B.2 – Service: Order processing

Overview	Provides support for all stages of the entering, fulfilling and subsequent invoicing of orders.
Available	At the desktop PCs of all staff who have registered with IS services as users of the service, and who have been authorised by Finance to process orders. The service is provided between 6am and 8pm, Monday–Friday, excluding public holidays at the HQ office. (A list of relevant public holidays is maintained at an appropriate intranet location.)
Authorisation	Authorisation to use the live service is to be arranged with Finance Services, email: finance@thiscompany.com, telephone 23456.
Training	On-line training packages for this service are available at training.location/order_processing.

B.4   Operational Risk Assessment

Risk assessments typically consider threats which may exploit vulnerabilities to impact the confidentiality, integrity or availability of one or more assets.

Operational Risk Assessments (ORAs) are specifically focused on risks associated with operational processes and systems.

Scope of an Operational Risk Assessment:

- identification of risks (threats and vulnerabilities)
- target, i.e. the assets under threat
- impact of risks, qualitative and quantitative
- probability of occurrence
- possible mitigating actions or controls
- identification of stakeholders who are
  - accountable for the risk, and responsible for selecting an appropriate action (including possibly accepting the risk with no control)
  - responsible for implementing selected actions or controls
- choice of actions or controls, based on evaluation of impact vs. cost of action or control.

For outsourced operations, particular care needs to be taken when considering the ownership of the assets at risk. These will be different for each party.

Risk Management processes need to be considered as cyclical, reviewing the suitability of previous actions, and reassessing risks in the light of changing circumstances.

Risks are likely to be managed through a risk register such as the example provided in Table B.3.

Table B.3 – Risk register

Ref.	Description	Weighted priority			Proposed actions or controls and costs	Owner
		Prob. HML	Impact HML	Prob. x Impact		
R1		H	H	9		
R2		H	M	6		
R3		M	L	3		
R4		L	L	I		

For further information on Risk Management, the OGC website defines a Risk framework and Risk Management processes, including specific considerations for Operational Risk Management.

www.ogc.gov.uk/sdtoolkit/workbooks/risk/index.html

Referenced from that site is a National Audit Office Risk Management report which provides considerable information on implementing effective Risk Management processes. Though primarily targeted at the public sector, it is also very applicable to the private sector, and draws examples from that sector.

www.ogc.gov.uk/sdtoolkit/reference/externalsources/naomanagrisk.pdf

B.5   Business Impact Analysis

The following templates are used to analyse/assess the impact on the business of any identified potential disruptions which may occur. The analysis is conducted against three areas:

- Resources needed to handle the disruption and return to normal service
- The impact in various areas of the identified disruptions
- Severity/criticality of the disruptions.

Table B.4 – Business Impact Analysis templates

Business Impact Analysis Identification of Resources Needed			159
Author	**Date**	**Document Name**	

Customer:	Function:	Process:	Review date:
			Page.... of....

Disruption	**Internal**	**External**	**Other**
	Property:	**Customers:**	
	Personnel:	**Suppliers:**	
	Equipment-HW:	**Potential Suppliers:**	
	Software:		
	Support:		

Disruption	**Internal**	**External**	**Other**
	Property:	**Customers:**	
	Personnel:	**Suppliers:**	
	Equipment-HW:	**Potential Suppliers:**	
	Software:		
	Support:		

Business Impact Analysis Impact Definition		
Author	**Date**	**Document Name**

Customer:	**Function:**	**Process:**	**Review date:**		
			Page.... of....		

Disruption	**Asset Loss**	**Continuity of:**	**Legal**	**Public Perception**	**Other**
	Physical:	Service:	Personal Data:	Customers:	
	Information:		Licences SW:	Suppliers:	
	Intangibles:	Operations:	Intellectual Property:	Potential customers:	
	Personnel:			Stock Exchange:	
	Physical:	Service:	Personal Data:	Customers:	
	Information:		Licences SW:	Suppliers:	
	Intangibles:	Operations:	Intellectual Property:	Potential customers:	
	Personnel:			Stock Exchange:	

Business Impact Analysis Severity/Criticality		
Author	Date	Document Name

Customer:	Function:	Process:		Review date:		
				Page.... of....		

Disruption	Quantitive:		Qualitative:	Severity	Criticality		Priority	
	Loss of Benefit:	Human Resources:	Human Resources:		Critical Support Functions:		Target Time:	
	Property Loss:	Additional Costs:	Legal:			Total Restart	Priority:	
	Fines:		Social:		Interdependency:		Target Time:	
	Cashflow:		Morale:			Partial Restart	Priority:	
	Legal Responsibility:		Confidence:					
Disruption	Quantitive:		Qualitative:	Severity	Criticality		Priority	
	Loss of Benefit:	Human Resources:	Human Resources:		Critical Support Functions:		Target Time:	
	Property Loss:	Additional Costs:	Legal:			Total Restart	Priority:	
	Fines:		Social:		Interdependency:		Target Time:	
	Cashflow:		Morale:			Partial Restart	Priority:	
	Legal Responsibility:		Confidence:					

APPENDIX C QUALITY

C.1   Quality Management

Quality Management for IT services is a systematic way of ensuring that all the activities necessary to design, develop and implement IT services which satisfy the requirements of the organisation and of users take place as planned and that the activities are carried out cost-effectively.

The way that an organisation plans to manage its operations so that it delivers quality services is specified by its Quality Management System. The Quality Management System defines the organisational structure, responsibilities, policies, procedures, processes, standards and resources required to deliver quality IT services. However, a Quality Management System will only function as intended if management and staff are committed to achieving its objectives.

This appendix gives brief details on a number of different Quality approaches – more detail on these and other approaches can be found on the Internet at www.dti.gov.uk/quality.

C.1.1   Deming

Quote

'We have learned to live in a world of mistakes and defective products as if they were necessary to life. It is time to adopt a new philosophy ...'

(W. Edwards Deming, 1900–1993)

W. Edwards Deming is best known for his management philosophy for establishing quality, productivity, and competitive position. As part of this philosophy, he formulated 14 points of attention for managers. Some of these points are more appropriate to Service Management than others.

For quality improvement Deming proposed the Deming Cycle or Circle. The four key stages are 'Plan, Do, Check and Act' after which a phase of consolidation prevents the 'Circle' from 'rolling down the hill' as illustrated in Figure C.1.

The cycle is underpinned by a process led approach to management where defined processes are in place, the activities measured for compliance to expected values and outputs audited to validate and improve the process.

Example

Excerpts from Deming's 14 points relevant to Service Management

- break down barriers between departments (improves communications and management)

- management must learn their responsibilities, and take on leadership (process improvement requires commitment from the top; good leaders motivate people to improve themselves and therefore the image of the organisation)

- improve constantly (a central theme for service managers is continual improvement; this is also a theme for Quality Management. A process led approach is key to achieve this target)

- institute a programme of education and self-improvement (learning and improving skills have been the focus of Service Management for many years)

- training on the job (linked to continual improvement)

- transformation is everyone's job (the emphasis being on teamwork and understanding).

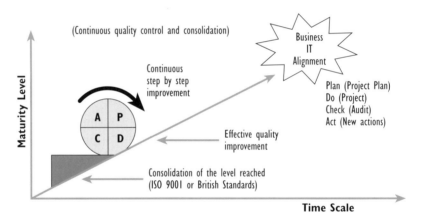

Figure C.1 – The Deming Cycle

C.1.2 Juran

Joseph Juran became a recognised name in the quality field in 1951 with the publication of the Quality Control Handbook. The appeal was to the Japanese initially, and Juran was asked to give a series of lectures in 1954 on planning, organisational issues, management responsibility for Quality, and the need to set goals and targets for improvement.

Juran devised a well-known chart, 'The Juran Trilogy', shown in Figure C.2, to represent the relationship between quality planning, quality control and quality improvement on a project-by-project basis.

A further feature of Juran's approach is the recognition of the need to guide managers; this is achieved by the establishment of a quality council within an organisation, which is responsible for establishing processes, nominating projects, assigning teams, making improvements and providing the necessary resources.

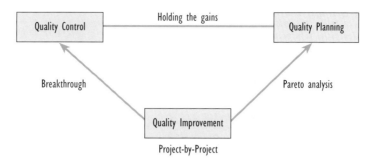

Figure C.2 – The Quality trilogy

Senior management plays a key role in serving on the quality council, approving strategic goals, allocating resources, and reviewing progress.

Juran promotes a four-phased approach to quality improvement, namely:

- Start-up – creating the necessary organisational structures and infrastructure

- Test – in which concepts are tried out in pilot programmes and results evaluated

- Scale-up – in which the basic concepts are extended based on positive feedback

- Institutionalisation – at which point quality improvements are linked to the strategic business plan.

C.1.3   Crosby

The Crosby TQM approach is very popular in the UK. However, despite its obvious success in the market, it has been subject to much criticism, primarily due to poor understanding, or a blinkered application of the approach in some organisations, using a limited definition of quality. The approach is based on Crosby's Four Absolutes of Quality Management, namely:

- Quality is conformance to requirement

- The system for causing quality is prevention and not appraisal

- The performance standard must be zero defects and not 'that's close enough'

- The measure of quality is the price of non-conformance and not indices.

The Crosby approach is often based on familiar slogans; however, organisations may experience difficulty in translating the quality messages into sustainable methods of quality improvement. Some organisations have found it difficult to integrate their quality initiatives, having placed their quality programme outside the mainstream management process.

Anecdotal evidence suggests that these pitfalls result in difficulties being experienced in sustaining active quality campaigns over a number of years in some organisations.

Crosby lacks the engineering rigour of Juran and significantly omits to design quality into the product or process, gearing the quality system towards a prevention-only policy. Furthermore, it fails to recognise that few organisations have appropriate management measures from which they can accurately ascertain the costs of non-conformance, and in some cases even the actual process costs!

C.1.4   Six Sigma

This is commonly described as a body of knowledge required to implement a generic quantitative approach to improvement. Six Sigma is a data-driven approach to analysing the root causes of problems and solving them. It is business output driven in relation to customer specification and focuses on dramatically reducing process variation using Statistical Process Control (SPC) measures. A process that operates at Six Sigma allows only 3.40 defects per million parts of output.

The Six Sigma approach has evolved from experience in manufacturing, and is therefore not readily applied to human processes and perhaps other processes that are not immediately apparent. The approach relies on trained personnel capable of identifying processes that need improvement and who can act accordingly. It does not contain a systematic approach for identifying improvement opportunities or facilitate with prioritisation.

Six Sigma perhaps offers another path toward measurable improvement for CMM Level 3 organisations, but this alone may make it difficult to apply in the context of Service Management compared to software engineering.

There are research reservations on applying validation and measurement to process improvement and particularly in the application of SPC to non-manufacturing engineering processes. It has been found that a Goal, Question, Metric (GQM) approach provides suitable measures, rather than a statistical method. It is still somewhat a controversial area, and even the SW-CMM at the higher levels (4–5) has come in for some academic criticism in this area. However, there are indications that Six Sigma is being applied in the service sector and, with good Service Management support tools, tracking of incidents, etc., this approach could be used for process improvement.

C.2 Formal quality initiatives

C.2.1 Quality standards

International Standards Organisation ISO 9000

An important set of International Standards for Quality Assurance is the ISO 9000 range, a set of five universal standards for a Quality Assurance system that is accepted around the world. At the turn of the millennium, 90 or so countries have adopted ISO 9000 as the cornerstone of their national standards. When a product or service is purchased from a company that is registered to the appropriate ISO 9000 standard, the purchaser has important assurances that the quality of what they will receive will be as expected.

The most comprehensive of the standards is ISO 9001. It applies to industries involved in the design, development, manufacturing, installation and servicing of products or services. The standards apply uniformly to companies in any industry and of any size.

The BSI Management Overview of IT Service Management is a modern update of the original document, PD0005, which was published in 1995. The Management Overview is a management level introduction to Service Management, and in fact can be used as an introduction to ITIL. This is also now supported by a formal standard, BS 15000 (Specification for IT Service Management). ITIL is in many countries the *de facto* standard and, with the help of BSI and ISO, it is hoped that a formal international standard based on ITIL will soon be in place. The BSI Standard and Management Overview cover the established ITIL Service Support and Service Delivery processes, as well as some additional topics such as implementing the processes.

C.2.2 Total Quality Systems: EFQM

Quote

'... the battle for Quality is one of the prerequisites for the success of your companies and for our collective success.'

(Jacques Delors, president of the European Commission, at the signing of the letter of intent in Brussels to establish EFQM on 15 September 1988)

The EFQM Excellence Model

The European Foundation for Quality Management (EFQM) was founded in 1988 by the Presidents of 14 major European companies, with the endorsement of the European Commission. The present membership is in excess of 600 very well-respected organisations, ranging from major multinationals and important national companies to research institutes in prominent European universities.

EFQM provides an excellent model for those wishing to achieve business excellence in a programme of continual improvement.

EFQM mission statement

The mission statement is:

> To stimulate and assist organisations throughout Europe to participate in improvement activities leading ultimately to excellence in customer satisfaction, employee satisfaction, impact on society and business results; and to support the Managers of European organisations in accelerating the process of making Total Quality Management a decisive factor for achieving global competitive advantage.

Depiction of the EFQM Excellence Model

The EFQM Excellence Model consists of 9 criteria and 32 sub-criteria; it is illustrated in Figure C.3.

In the model there is explicit focus on the value to users of the 'Plan, Do, Check, Act' cycle to business operations (see Section C.1.1), and the need to relate everything that is done, and the measurements taken, to the goals of business policy and strategy.

Self-assessment and maturity: the EFQM maturity scale

One of the tools provided by EFQM is the self-assessment questionnaire. The self-assessment process allows the organisation to discern clearly its strengths and also any areas where improvements can be made. The questionnaire process culminates in planned improvement actions, which are then monitored for progress.

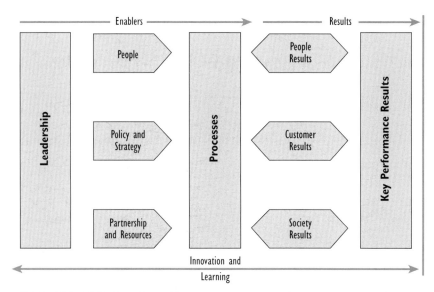

©EFQM. The EFQM Excellence Model is a registered trademark

Figure C.3 – The EFQM Excellence Model

In this assessment progress can be checked against a five-point maturity scale:

1 Product orientation

2 Process orientation (the maturity stage aimed for by the original ITIL)

3 System orientation (the maturity target for ITIL-compliant organisations in the new millennium)

4 Chain orientation

5 Total quality.

C.2.3 Quality awards

To demonstrate a successful adaptation of the EFQM model, some companies aim for the European Quality Award, a process that allows Europe to recognise its most successful organisations and promote them as role models of excellence for others to copy.

The US equivalent to this award is the Malcolm Baldridge Quality Award for Quality Management. The Malcolm Baldridge National Quality Improvement Act of 1987 established an annual US National Quality Award. The purpose of the Award was (and still is) to promote awareness of quality excellence, to recognise quality achievements of US companies, and to publicise successful quality strategies.

For the Malcolm Baldridge Award, there are three categories:

■ Manufacturing companies or sub-units

■ Service companies or sub-units

■ Small businesses.

The criteria against which firms are judged are:

1 Leadership

2 Strategic planning

3   Customer and market focus

4   Information and analysis

5   Human resource development and management

6   Process management

7   Business results.

For the European Quality Award, there are four possible categories:

- Companies
- Operational units of companies
- Public sector organisations
- Small and medium enterprises.

The criteria against which candidate organisations are measured are:

1   Leadership

2   People

3   Policy and strategy

4   Partnerships and resources

5   Processes

6   People results

7   Customer results

8   Society results

9   Key performance results.

In the EFQM Excellence Model, the first four criteria are defined as enablers. Best practice in ITIL process implementations show that placing proper emphasis on these topics increases the chances for success. The key points for the four enablers are listed below.

Leadership

- Organise a kick-off session involving everyone
- Be a role model
- Encourage and support the staff.

People management

- Create awareness
- Recruit new staff and/or hire temporary staff to prevent Service Levels being affected during implementation stages
- Develop people through training and experience
- Align human resource plans with policy and strategy
- Adopt a coaching style of management
- Align performance with salaries.

Policy and strategy

- Communicate mission, vision and values
- Align communication plans with the implementation stages.

Partnerships and resources

- Establish partnerships with subcontractors and customers
- Use financial resources in support of policy and strategy
- Utilise existing assets.

INDEX

Other Information Sources and Services

The IT Service Management Forum (itSMF)

The IT Service Management Forum Ltd (itSMF) is the only internationally recognised and independent body dedicated to IT Service Management. It is a not-for-profit organisation, wholly owned, and principally operated, by its membership.

The itSMF is a major influence on, and contributor to, Industry Best Practice and Standards worldwide, working in partnership with OGC (the owners of ITIL), the British Standards Institution (BSI), the Information Systems Examination Board (ISEB) and the Examination Institute of the Netherlands (EXIN).

How to contact us:

The IT Service Management Forum Ltd
Webbs Court
8 Holmes Road
Earley
Reading RG6 7BH
Tel: +44 (0) 118 926 0888
Fax: +44 (0) 118 926 3073
Email: service@itsmf.com
or visit our web-site at:
www.itsmf.com

Founded in the UK in 1991, there are now a number of chapters around the world with new ones seeking to join all the time. There are well in excess of 1000 organisations covering over 10,000 individuals represented in the membership. Organisations range from large multi-nationals such as AXA, GuinnessUDV, HP, Microsoft and Procter & Gamble in all market sectors, through central & local bodies, to independent consultants.

ITIL training and professional qualifications

For further information:

visit ISEB's web-site at:
www.bcs.org.uk

and EXIN:
www.exin.nl

There are currently two examining bodies offering equivalent qualifications: ISEB (The Information Systems Examining Board), part of the British Computer Society, and Stitching EXIN (The Netherlands Examinations Institute). Jointly with OGC and itSMF (the IT Service Management Forum), they work to ensure that a common standard is adopted for qualifications worldwide. The syllabus is based on the core elements of ITIL and complies with ISO9001 Quality Standard. Both ISEB and EXIN also accredit training organisations to deliver programmes leading to qualifications.

Best Practice:

the OGC approach with ITIL® and PRINCE®

OGC Best Practice is an approach to management challenges as well as the application of techniques and actions.

Practical, flexible and adaptable, management guidance from OGC translates the very best of the world's practices into guidance of an internationally recognised standard. Both PRINCE2 and ITIL publications can help every organisation to:

- Run projects more efficiently
- Reduce project risk
- Purchase IT more cost effectively
- Improve organisational Service Delivery.

What is ITIL and why use it?

ITIL's starting point is that organisations do not simply use IT; they depend on it. Managing IT as effectively as possible must therefore be a high priority.

ITIL consists of a unique library of guidance on providing quality IT services. It focuses tightly on the customer, cost effectiveness and building a culture that puts the emphasis on IT performance.

Used by hundreds of the world's most successful organisations, its core titles are available in print, Online Subscription and CD-ROM formats. They are:

- Service Support
- Service Delivery
- Planning to Implement Service Management
- Application Management
- ICT Infrastructure Management
- Security Management
- The Business Perspective Volume 1 and 2
- Software Asset Management

What is PRINCE2 and why use it?

Since its introduction in 1989, PRINCE has been widely adopted by both the public and private sectors and is now recognised as a de facto standard for project management – and for the management of change.

PRINCE2, the most evolved version, is driven by its experts and users to offer control, transparency, focus and ultimate success for any project you need to implement.

Publications are available in various formats: print, Online Subscription and CD-ROM. Its main titles are:

- Managing Successful Projects with PRINCE2
- People Issues and PRINCE2
- PRINCE2 Pocket Book
- Tailoring PRINCE2
- Business Benefits through Project Management

Other related titles:
- Passing the PRINCE2 Examinations
- Managing Successful Programmes
- Management of Risk – Guidance for Practitioners
- Buying Software – A best practice approach

Ordering

The full range of ITIL and PRINCE2 publications can be purchased direct via **www.get-best-practice.co.uk** or through calling TSO Customer Services on **0870 600 5522**. If you are outside of the UK please contact your local agent, for details email **sales@tso.co.uk** For information on Network Licenses for CD-ROM and Online Subscription please email **network.sales@tso.co.uk**

You are also able to subscribe to content online through this website or by calling TSO Customer Services on **0870 600 5522**. For more information on how to subscribe online please refer to our help pages on the website.

Dear customer ■ ■ ■ ■ ■ ■ ■ ■ ■ ■ ■ ■ ■ ■ □

We would like to hear from you with any comments or suggestions that you have on how we can improve our current products or develop new ones for the ITIL series. Please complete this questionnaire and we will enter you into our quarterly draw. The winner will receive a copy of Software Asset Management worth £35!

1 Personal Details

Name ....

Organisation ....

Job Title ....

Department ....

Address ....

....

Postcode ....

Telephone Number ....

Email ....

2 Nature of Organisation (tick one box only)

☐ Consultancy/Training
☐ Computing/IT/Software
☐ Industrial
☐ Central Government
☐ Local Government
☐ Academic/Further education
☐ Private Health
☐ Public Health (NHS)
☐ Finance
☐ Construction
☐ Telecommunications
☐ Utilities
☐ Other (Please specify)

....

3 How did you hear about **ITIL?**

☐ Work/Colleagues
☐ Internet/Web (please specify)

....

☐ Marketing Literature
☐ itSMF
☐ Other (please specify)

....

4 Where did you purchase this book?

☐ Web – www.tso.co.uk/bookshop
☐ Web – www.get-best-practice.co.uk
☐ Web – Other (please specify)

....

☐ Bookshop (please specify)

....

☐ Training Course
☐ Other (please specify)

....

5 How many people use **ITIL** in your company?

☐ 1-5
☐ 6-10
☐ 11-50
☐ 51-200
☐ 201+

6 How many people use your copy of this title?

☐ 0
☐ 1-5
☐ 6-10
☐ 11+

7 Overall, how do you rate this title?

☐ Excellent
☐ Very Good
☐ Good
☐ Fair
☐ Poor

8 What do you most like about the book? (tick all that apply)

☐ Ease of use
☐ Well structured
☐ Contents
☐ Index
☐ Hints and tips
☐ Other (Please specify)

....

9 Do you have any suggestions for improvement?

....

....

....

....

10 How do you use this book? (tick all that apply)

☐ Problem Solver
☐ Reference
☐ Tutorial
☐ Other (please specify)

....

[PTO]

11 Did you know there are 7 core titles in the **ITIL** series?

☐ No
☐ Yes

12 Do you have any other **ITIL** titles?

☐ No
☐ Yes (please specify)

....

13 Do you use the **ITIL** CDs?

☐ No
☐ Yes (please specify)

....

14 Are you aware that most of the **ITIL** series is now available as online content at **www.get-best-practice.co.uk?**

☐ Yes
☐ No

15 Do you currently subscribe to any online content found at **www.get-best-practice.co.uk?**

☐ No
☐ Yes (please specify)

....

16 Did you know that you can network your CDs and Online Subscription, to offer your project managers access to this material at their desktop?

Yes/No

☐ Please tick this box if you require further information.

17 Did you know that you are able to purchase a maintenance agreement for your CD-ROM that will allow you to receive immediately any revised versions, at no additional cost?

Yes/No

☐ Please tick this box if you require further information.

18 What business change guidance/methods does your company use?

☐ PRINCE2
☐ Managing Successful Programmes
☐ Management of Risk
☐ Successful Delivery Toolkit
☐ Business Systems Development (BSD)
☐ Other (please specify)

....

19 What is the job title of the person who makes the decision to implement **ITIL** and/or purchase IT?

....

....

20 Which three websites do you visit the most?

1 ....

2 ....

3 ....

21 Which 3 professional magazines do you read the most?

1 ....

2 ....

3 ....

22 Will you be attending any events or conferences this year related to IT, if so, which?

....

To enter your Questionnaire into our monthly draw please return this form to our Freepost Address:

**Marketing – ITIL Questionnaire
TSO
Freepost ANG4748
Norwich
NR3 1YX**

The ITIL series is available in a range of formats: hard copy, CD-ROM and now available as an Online Subscription. For further details and to purchase visit **www.get-best-practice.co.uk**

Any further enquiries or questions about ITIL or the Office of Government Commerce should be directed to the OGC Service Desk:

The OGC Service Desk
Rosebery Court
St Andrews Business Park
Norwich
NR7 0HS

Email: ServiceDesk@ogc.gsi.gov.uk
Telephone: 0845 000 4999

TSO will not sell, rent or pass any of your details onto interested third parties. The details you supply will be used for market research purposes only and to keep you up to date with TSO products and services which we feel maybe of interest to you. **If you would like us to use your information to keep you updated please indicate how you would like us to communicate with you:**

Telephone ☐   Email ☐   Mail ☐